THE DANCERS INHERIT THE PARTY

Early Stories, Plays and Poems

Ian Hamilton Finlay

THE DANCERS INHERIT THE PARTY

Early Stories, Plays and Poems

Edited and introduced by
Ken Cockburn

in association with

SCOTTISH POETRY LIBRARY
By leaves we live

First published in Great Britain in 2004 by
Polygon (an imprint of Birlinn Ltd)
in association with the Scottish Poetry Library
West Newington House
10 Newington Road
Edinburgh
EH9 1QS

www.birlinn.co.uk
www.spl.org.uk

ISBN 1 904598 13 7

Scottish
Arts Council

The publishers acknowledge subsidy from the
Scottish Arts Council towards the publication of this volume.

British Library Cataloguing-in-Publication Data
A catalogue record for this book is
available on request from the British Library

Typeset by Hewer Text, Edinburgh
Printed and bound by
Creative Print and Design, Ebbw Vale, Wales

Contents

A Note on the Text   vii
Foreword by Robert Creeley   xi
Introduction by Ken Cockburn   xiii

Stories
in order of date of publication

Break for Tea   3
The Blue-Coated Fishermen   5
The Two Fishermen   13
Fisher by the Stove   20
Boy with Wheel   25
The Sea-Bed   29
Midsummer Weather   36
The Slim, Grey Beauty   38
The Potato Planters and the Old Joiner's Funeral   44
The Old Man and the Trout   49
The Fight in the Ditch   55
Over the Sharp Stones   60
Advice from the Author   65
Encounter   70
The Old Fisherman   75
The Money   82
The Boy and the Guess   90
Straw   94
Pills   99
A Broken Engagement   105
The Potato Field   109

Plays

The Estate Hunters   117
Walking Through Seaweed   137
The Wild Dogs in Winter   153

Poems

The Dancers Inherit the Party   173
Glasgow Beasts, An a Burd   217

Uncollected Poems   237
Bibliography   245

A Note on the Text

This volume reprints all the poems in *The Dancers Inherit the Party* and *Glasgow Beasts, an a Burd*, published in one volume by Polygon (1996), and the foreword to that edition by Robert Creeley. It also includes additional uncollected poems and a selection of plays and short stories from the period 1951–1962.

The material from the 1996 Polygon edition includes all but two of the poems from the original Migrant Press edition of *The Dancers Inherit the Party*, which appeared in November 1960 (a new edition appeared in 1962). The third edition, published by Fulcrum Press (London) in 1969, included seven new poems – 'The Tug', 'End of a Holiday', 'The One-Horse Town', 'Poet', 'Scene', 'Art Student', and 'Snow in Rousay', Finlay's response to 'Snow' by the Japanese poet, Miyoshi – which were written between 1961 and 1966, and appeared in various little magazines and anthologies, most notably Cid Corman's *Origin* (II.6: Kyoto, 1962). A dispute arose because the book was wrongly described as a first edition, and, after a protracted legal case, the complete edition was withdrawn. *Glasgow Beasts, An A Burd* was first published by Finlay's own Wild Flounder Press (a nautical sister to the Wild Hawthorn Press) in 1961. The second edition appeared in February 1962, the third edition in June 1962, the fourth edition in December of the same year and the fifth edition was published by Fulcrum Press in 1965.

The additional uncollected poems in this volume are 'Fishing from the Back of Rousay' from *Lines Review* (no. 17: Edinburgh, 1961); and 'Poem on my poem on her and the horse', 'Such is the world', 'Zukofsky/Finlay', 'Lucky', 'The Village Baker', 'Midhope (all gone)' and 'Dalchonzie' from *Origin*.

The selected stories reprinted here were first printed in newspapers and journals. 'Break for Tea' (October 1952), 'The Blue-Coated Fishermen' (March 1953), 'The Two Fishermen' (June 1953), 'The Sea-Bed' (August 1953) and 'The Old Man and the Trout' (November 1953) were first printed in *The Scottish Angler*, which was edited by the poet Crombie Saunders. 'Fisher by the Stove' (13 June 1953), 'Boy with Wheel' (18 July 1953), 'Midsummer Weather' (22 August 1953), 'The Slim, Grey Beauty' (12 September 1953), 'The Potato Planters and the Old Joiner's Funeral' (printed 24 October 1953 as 'The Potato Planters'), 'The Fight in the Ditch' (28 November 1953), 'Over the Sharp Stones' (26 December 1953), 'Advice from the Author' (17 April 1954), 'Encounter' (15 May 1954), 'The Old Fisherman' (14 August 1954), 'The Money' (printed 25 September 1954 as 'National Assistance Money'), 'The Boy and the Guess' (29 January 1955), 'Pills' (28 May 1955), 'A Broken Engagement' (3 September 1955) and 'The Potato Field' (15 October 1955) were first published in *The Glasgow Herald*. 'Straw' was first published in *Scotland's Magazine*, May 1955.

Of the selection reprinted here, those later included in *The Sea-Bed and Other Stories* (Edinburgh: Castle Wynd Printers, 1958) were 'The Potato Planters and the Old Joiner's Funeral', 'The Sea-Bed', 'The Old Man and the Trout', 'The Money' (as 'National Assistance Money'), 'The Boy and the Guess', 'Straw', 'Pills' and 'A Broken Engagement'.

The plays 'The Estate Hunters' and 'Walking Through Seaweed' are reprinted from *New English Dramatists 14* (Harmondsworth: Penguin Books, 1970). 'The Wild Dogs in Winter' is printed from an unpublished playscript from the personal collection of Lesley Lendrum.

Further material in the Introduction to this volume came from the Ian Hamilton Finlay Collection in the National Library of Scotland.

Lesley Lendrum provided invaluable help in the preparation of this book, as did the librarians at the National Library of Scotland

and the Scottish Theatre Archive. Lilias Fraser at the Scottish Poetry Library helped research the additional material for this edition from newspapers and archive material and other sources. The 1996 edition mentioned above was edited by Alec Finlay, to whom the editor of this volume extends particular thanks for his advice and for his encouragement. The second paragraph above was originally written by him for the 1996 edition. Thanks are also due to Ian Hamilton Finlay for his support of this edition of his early works and for his helpful consideration of the Introduction.

Foreword*

I've always felt that Ian Hamilton Finlay's genius, for once the apt word, had altogether to do with his being particularly in a place, whether the loftlike apartment on Fettes Row in Edinburgh where we first met in 1964, or, in the years that followed, his singular invention of Little Sparta where all his art has now found a home. In that earlier time he did not move easily in public spaces, albeit he confounded them nonetheless with all manner of wit and device, from the familiar letter to *The Times* to paper gliders and kites whereon he wrote his succinct messages to a seemingly blind world. No doubt it brought him small respect, yet he was certainly a brilliantly insistent presence. He had such a deft, quick humour, always alert, wry, various, but with gentleness. His work has never been casual if by that one means the drift of chance and affections. He has been directed by what he believed himself capable of doing, and has done it in each instance with fiercely specific determination.

One must never forget that poets are *makers*, most vividly so in Scotland, where William Dunbar's 'Lament for the Makaris' must still echo with uncanny poignance. Poetry is 'a made thing', as Robert Duncan put it. No poet will ever manage a word, much less a line, without all the resources of that art in timeless history sounding there, as each word finds its place in turn. There is no way to learn simply the intimacy of voice that Finlay has always, bringing one in to his physical person. It is a constant of his art in all its forms. Thus 'The Dancers Inherit the Party' is one of the

* This foreword was written for the 1996 edition of *The Dancers Inherit the Party*

most elegant poems I've ever read, so clear in what it says and how it says it, so physically, words' pace and sound.

Then why did he not go on making these affectionate, compelling, masterful wee beauties – these songs of our common lives? He did, in fact, but the *things* changed, call them, turned to stone and water, words as image or name or simply trace in mind of a reflection. For years I've mulled over the source of a tag in Pound's *Cantos*, which can be translated, *The grove demands an altar* – or *wants*, or *needs* ('vult nemus aram'). The physical world *needs* an acknowledgement, a prayer, a faith, a place for its recognition. I think of Ian Finlay as the great classicist of this commitment to wonder and surmise, to 'A small rise, over which the top of a mast and sail may be glimpsed, suggesting the sea.'

ROBERT CREELEY

Introduction

This book of stories, plays and poems is an Ian Hamilton Finlay reader from what one might call the strictly literary part of his career. It includes short stories written by Finlay from the late 1940s through to the mid-1950s, plays written in the late 1950s, and two poem-sequences and several uncollected poems from the early 1960s. By 1963 Finlay had largely ceased using conventional literary forms and begun writing concrete poetry, which led directly a few years later to the poem-objects and sculptural works featured at Little Sparta, the renowned garden in Lanarkshire which he developed from 1966 with his second wife, Sue. It is fascinating to look at the early works included here, and relate their exploration of the pastoral, of conflict, of making a home in the world, to Finlay's later achievements at Little Sparta.

Born in 1925, Finlay's early years were spent in the Bahamas, where his father lucratively ran bootleg alcohol into Prohibition-era USA. At the age of six he was sent to Scotland to boarding school, first to Larchfield School near Helensburgh, then to Dollar Academy. After the repeal of prohibition in 1933, his parents moved into the legal business of orange growing in Florida which, ironically, ruined them and forced their return to Scotland. The family lived, in restricted circumstances, in Glasgow, while Finlay holidayed in a cottage near Hopetoun House to the west of Edinburgh, with an aunt and her brother, who was a night watchman at the 'big house'. Good-sized trout were to be fished from a nearby burn. After the outbreak of World War Two, he was evacuated to rural Perthshire.

The first written reference to Finlay comes in a letter of 10

January 1943 written by Hugh MacDiarmid to the bookseller, Charles Lahr: 'my purpose . . . is to introduce a young friend of mine, Ian Finlay, who is anxious to find a congenial job of some kind in London, – a job in a book-shop, or with some publishing firm, or in journalism.' The next couple of years were spent partly in Glasgow, where he got to know the poet W. S. Graham, and in London, where he met Dylan Thomas and the 'two Roberts', Colquhoun and MacBryde. Between 1945 and 1947 he undertook National Service, initially with the Non-Combatant Corps, and then with the Royal Army Service Corps, where he rose to the rank of sergeant. Posted to Germany, his duties included liasing between Poles who found themselves in the British sector, and the emergent German civil authorities. The posting prompted the short, unpublished essay 'Autobahn Aesthetic':

In the bewildering series of impressions to which the tourist – even the anonymous, disciplined tourist in khaki – is subject, none, however, impressed me more than the sight of this amazing road which thrust, in arrow-flights of effortless curves, across the hills. (. . .) Technically, aesthetically, it is a superb creation, but its very excellence attests to a technical proficiency which has its drawbacks – a weak word with which to indicate the spectacle of destruction that is Germany today. We in the West are justly proud of our unprecedented technical skill: we face a crisis in which it will be shown whether our scientific advances are ultimately reconcilable with a peace-giving conception of the destiny of man.

For some time he was based at Paderborn, where the Germans had maintained a Panzer training centre, and where British tanks were now stationed. These were housed in fine neo-classical buildings, undamaged by the war. If the combination of modern military technology and classical landscape in such later works as 'Footnotes to an Essay' (1977, with Guy Hincks and Stephen Bann) seems like a post-modern conceit, it is worth remembering their grounding in a historical reality directly experienced by Finlay. 'The Third Reich Revisited' (1982, with Ian Appleton) also attempts to admire the technical and aesthetic achievements of Nazi (and neo-classical) architecture – intact and in ruins – while now consciously 'de-Nazifying' them by incorporating short texts to shift their meaning away from German political expansionism towards a sense of 'The Beyond, The Infinite, the Immeasurable'. In 1948 Finlay was again living in rural Perthshire, at Drum-na-Keil near Comrie, with his first wife Marion. (MacDiarmid was best man at the wedding.) He spent the next few years in rural poverty, writing and painting while earning money by piece-work, before being hospitalised in 1954 as the result of a breakdown. At the end of the following year he was building a road on the island of Rousay in Orkney, and his marriage was breaking up. Between 1956 and 1964 he lived mostly in Edinburgh.

By the early 1960s he had fallen out publicly with MacDiarmid, by way of the so-called 'Honour'd Shade flyting'. Finlay and several other younger writers were annoyed at their exclusion from the anthology Honour'd Shade, edited by Norman MacCaig. They produced a recording and an event, both called 'Dishonoured Shade'; a 'flyting' was conducted in the letters pages of The Scotsman, and MacDiarmid concluded his side of the debate with an abusive pamphlet, the ugly birds without wings (1962). Finlay, on the other hand, arranged 'a huge protest march with banners by avant garde artists', which was never intended actually to take place and which he later described as 'entirely mythological'. It had nonetheless the desired effect, with the issue being taken seriously and discussed by many people, some of whom later claimed to have witnessed the march. In 1961 Finlay founded, with Jessie McGuffie, the magazine Poor.Old.Tired.Horse, which was to run for twenty five numbers until 1967. Its title, taken from the poem 'Please' by Robert Creeley, reflects Finlay's increasing interest in American writing – his work around this time has been described as 'beat kailyard' – but the magazine published a broad and eclectic range of writers, from Scots 'traditionalists' such as Robert Garioch and George Mackay Brown, to European and American avant-gardists such as Eugen Gomringer and Jerome Rothenberg. It also featured work by visual artists like Bridget Riley and John Furnival, and brought Finlay into direct contact with a much wider world of literature and art. The year 1961 also saw the founding of the Wild Hawthorn Press and the publication of pamphlets and posters by writers and artists Finlay admired, such as Lorine Niedecker, Augusto de Campos and Victor Vasarely. Increasingly, however, it became the imprint under which Finlay produced the astounding array of printed material that complemented his development of Little Sparta, and the worldwide commissions he came to receive as a result of his garden's fame.

It is perhaps worth mentioning that from the early 1960s until recently his agoraphobia prevented him travelling, so his publications formed a crucial part of his engagement with the wider world. Both *P.O.T.H.* and Wild Hawthorn Press emerged from a need to define an art and aesthetics separate from MacDiarmid and his influence, and to create a 'support structure' of like-minded practitioners, though as noted above this was the opposite of closed and exclusive. It is also worth mentioning the folk revival, pioneered by Hamish Henderson, with which Finlay engaged to an extent in his poems at the time, but soon moved on from into 'concrete'.

Broadly speaking, during the two decades from the late 1940s to the late 1960s, Finlay moved sequentially from painting to short stories, to plays, to poems, to concrete poems, to poem-objects, to the garden where, in a sense, everything came together. By this I mean that the rural landscapes described in the stories became real landscapes into which people entered to contemplate, converse, and to enact certain events like a piece of theatre; these activities and the landscape were informed by short texts, the poems in their most reduced form. It is the shifts in form, rather than in subject matter, which give the clearest indication of Finlay's progress through these years. They mark not a disenchantment with any particular form, or sense of failure, but instead provide an impulse to further development. As he wrote to Derek Stanford in 1967, when he was very much considered a concrete poet:

> I am very keen on concrete poetry, but some of the delight has gone . . . partly because I always feel most enthusiastic when making fresh starts in a state of total innocence. (. . .) The fact is, though, that my basic ideas have never really changed; I still see art as being to do with order and some kind of ethical plain-ness.

Of the short stories included here, several appeared in a booklet published in 1958, *The Sea-Bed and Other Stories*, while the remainder appeared in newspapers and magazines in the four years between December 1951 and December 1955. Certain stories, particularly 'The Money' and 'A Broken Engagement', have become known through their appearance in anthologies, but most have not been reprinted since the 1950s. This selection is made from stories found in the course of preparing this edition, but it is likely that there are other stories as yet uncatalogued.

All of the stories either have entirely rural settings, or feature a journey to or from the countryside. Most take place over a single day or less, some almost take place in 'real-time' or the time of their telling. The earliest 'stories' are in fact more or less descriptive essays, without character or plot, as if Finlay were first having to articulate the world in which his stories would take place, before he could people such a world, and present human activity within it. Many stories involve fishing, others involve farm-work. A rather impractical but not incapable artist-figure narrates several stories, but he accepts, and is accepted by, the more down-to-earth figures around him. He is drawn perhaps, from the Russian literary tradition, sharing aspects of the well-meaning but ineffectual landowner and the fiery but marginalised artist one might find in a story by Chekov or Turgenev.

Other stories focus on children, often boys aged around twelve, whose attitude to the world is similar to the artist's: capable of engagement with it, without having to take responsibility for material or economic production. Both have a certain freedom to appreciate the world simply as it is, without anxiety as how best to exploit it for gain. It is a limited world, but Finlay saw this as no disadvantage, as he wrote to J. F. Hendry in December 1955:

I see, now, it is possible to make any kind of story a fishing story. (. . .) Universal problems treated in particular terms. Around incidents they settle, and that is the start of a story. There is a whole world in Perthshire that is as unique as Faulkner's Deep South – no-one is aware of it. No writers I mean.

'Sadness' is a recurring mood or emotion, but refers less to a sense of loss or failure, than to a state of heightened sensitivity when the beauty and purity of the world are perceived; beauty and purity which are, however, distant, unattainable and inexpressible. In 'A Broken Engagement', as each evening Peggy, the maid, draws the boy a face, the mood is one of a permanent sunset. Such beauty for the boy both transcends and limits the world around him: it offers an experience of intimacy beyond what he is used to within his family, yet it also fixes the way he relates to Peggy, so that she becomes merely the means to an end. The narrator seems to be using the narrative to describe his younger self's delight and ignorance, the latter the sympton of a deadening of curiosity caused by the former.

One of the stories' great strengths is the evocation of place and atmosphere; the light at a particular time of day, or the oppressive anticipation of an approaching storm. But this idea that beauty can be perceived most intensely by an individual at a particular moment, rather than shared communally or socially as it unfolds over a period of time, leads to something of a cul-de-sac.

In several stories, wee fish are caught, cooked and eaten with relish. But the big fish are problematic. In 'The Sea-Bed', the boy's momentary sighting of the cod-fish is enough to disturb him profoundly, but also to satisfy him. He has no need to catch the fish to prove anything, indeed the thought of catching it makes him anxious. The tools available to the more ambitious fishermen in these stories are however incapable of landing large fish. Having swallowed the inadequate hook or broken the inadequate line, they swim out of the fishermen's reach to their deaths, which evoke a range of emotional responses from the stories' protagonists. The boy in 'The Old Man and the Trout', largely unaware of the old man's caution when they go fishing, or rather poaching, instinctively understands enough of the old man's regret at what has happened not to speak to him about finding the dead trout. The fisherman in *The Slim, Grey Beauty* refers to the trout of his desire, who casually ignores his baited hook, as a 'hoor', and there is an aspect of sexual attraction and aggression in his attitude to the fish, made explicit when he compares it to 'a grey, half-naked foreign girl, crouching', seen during his war service. The trout's subsequent escape and death he regards with little more than indifference. But the most brutal reaction to 'beauty' is described in 'The Fight in the Ditch', when Big Dod, the farm-worker, kills the trout and breaks its body to pieces with his bare hands, because he perceives it as an enemy and a threat to himself, as if allowing such a substantial creature to retain its freedom would point up his own limitations. Perhaps he sees it as something forbidden to him, the prerogative of men rich enough to afford fishing-permits, or indeed to own the estate itself. Whatever the case, he cannot let it be.

'Fittingness' is a quality much valued in the stories, as it continues to be throughout Finlay's career. It is a state of affairs in which beings, and things, are allowed to be themselves, and are appreciated as themselves, without being contained, distorted, exploited or owned by another. There is a suspicion of authority, which by its nature appears to distort people's characters, as any authority they have is dependent on others, and forces them to act within confines which they themselves cannot define. The gamekeeper's rage in 'Encounter'; the Famous Author's broken promises in 'Advice from the Author'; the Labour Exchange officials' attitudes in 'The Money'; in each case their authority causes an imbalance in their relationship with others.

Conflict, when it occurs in the stories, remains largely unspoken. In 'Over the Sharp Stones' the old man does not confront the gamekeeper about the gin-traps, but secretly steals them each time they are set, and replaces them with his own snares. The city workman's defiance of the gamekeeper in 'Encounter' is largely silent. The response of the artist narrator in 'The Money' to the complicated regulations of officialdom is to say simply, 'I resign', and to work outwith the system. This story is oddly prescient of Finlay's long-running dispute with Strathclyde Regional Council, over whether his 'Garden Temple' could be designated a religious building. Again, there was a problem of categorising an artist's activities, but this time Finlay did not resign but fight and make work out of the fight, which he named the 'Little Spartan Wars'. In the end though, at least legally, the Council prevailed.

The corollary of conflict, friendship, also remains largely unspoken. It is expressed most succinctly at the end of 'The Sea-Bed', and also at the end of the play *Walking Through Seaweed*, when the two boys and the two girls respectively, though the chasm of misunderstanding between them is vast, are able to link arms and walk together to a shared social destination, the village or the café. Finlay wrote to J. F. Hendry in 1956 or 1957 that:

'The Sea-Bed' interests me because it seems to be about my breakdown, long before I knew the experience; and also, the ending proposes the only solution I can see. Which is, namely, one of tenderness – that people must gang up against the void, as the only consolation. There is only the 'thin, warm arm', which is sex, and tenderness, and friendship.

The first step on from the stories was writing plays for the stage and for broadcast on radio. Inevitably the writer's isolation is ended, as he is forced to work with a range of people to realise the work. When produced, it exists not on the page but in the world; in a theatre, or wherever the radio is found. The setting has to be evoked, visually or aurally, for the audience, and can no longer be directly imparted to them by the author, by way of description. Initially Finlay seems to have found this difficult, as he wrote to J F Hendry:

Drama? Well, I wrote a one-act play, but it was a disaster. For one thing, it somehow came to include 2,000 sheep. Also, I required a page of stage-directions in order to make one character say – for instance – 'pass the salt'. In short, I like to say what is going on inside the people, rather than to make it appear.

'The Estate-Hunters', in comparison with 'Straw', the story on which it is based, rather loses in poignancy, as the fact of the father's impending death, mentioned near the start of the story and consequently colouring all that happens, is impossible to bring into the play without some kind of structural modification. There is an almost Victorian sentimentality to the off-stage dying horse, presented as a static fact, and it's interesting to relate this to the alive and talking coal-horse at the end of *Glasgow Beasts*. Otherwise, while its depiction of the characters' relationship is well realised, and it does not feature 2,000 sheep, it would be challenging to stage, with three scenes taking place simply enough in a flat in Glasgow, but the fourth requiring 'in the foreground, a burn with a pool; in the background, pine trees and an old stone bridge'. While radio allows for a greater variety of setting than the stage, the visual detail given here suggests a more specific place than might be suggested by the sound of a burn running over pebbles.

'Walking Through Seaweed' uses the possibilities and ambiguities of stage action more simply and more fully. Similar in many ways to 'The Sea-Bed', it develops the perception of uncanny beauty experienced by the main character in that story, while granting a voice to the other character who is unable to share the vision. The result is a move away from the story's vivid description of place, to the exploration of a relationship, of the clash of priorities which the two girls have, and at the same time an enactment of Finlay's call for tenderness and friendship – the two girls have to keep talking, even as they disagree, or fail to understand one another's point of view. The play's setting is the street, a neutral public space midway between the girls' homes and their destination, the café, where presumably they will meet with others of their own age. The 'beauty' evoked – the sensation of walking barefoot through seaweed – is more ordinary, more achievable and more sensually direct than the sight of the large cod-fish. Finlay is also able to explore more fully in dramatic form the uncertainty and the ambiguity of the feelings evoked by beauty, as reading or watching the play one is never sure whether this is an actual or imagined experience, just as one is never sure whether the girls do or don't have the boyfriends they speak about. There is lightness, a wistfulness, present now. The play is much more engaged with the modern world than the stories, with its shop windows, café and pop songs, indeed its whole evocation of the 'teenager', at that point still a very new concept.

'The Wild Dogs in Winter' on the other hand moves away from the 'realist romantic style' of the stories towards outright symbolism. While few of the characters in the stories are granted names, they are discernibly individuals, whereas in this play they are reduced to types, playing out pre-ordained roles, fixed within the confines of those roles. Again, the specific setting is unimportant, becoming a backdrop to the dramatic action, which develops the destructive violence explored in 'The Fight in the Ditch'. At the end of that story Big Dod goes back to work, alone and satisfied, but does not interact with others. Here, one who has carried out an act of destructive violence is placed among other people, revelling in his act which they are either unable or unwilling to detect. Still, conflict remains unchallenged.

The shift to poetry marks a move away from the description of landscape in the stories, and the depiction of relationships in the plays, towards formalism, concision and transformation. Certain poems in *The Dancers* take themes already familiar from the stories: 'Optimist', for example, like the earlier 'Break for Tea', is about brewing tea in a billy-can, while 'Black Tomintoul' develops the difficult sexuality of the stories, switching now to a female voice which is both more aware of her feelings and less inclined to destructiveness. Rather than relying on description, however lucid or exact it might be, the poems put the subject matter in the background, and foreground instead the movement of thought, conveyed by formal means, principally rhythm and rhyme. It might be a more conventional career-path for a writer to move from the short story, not to the lyric, but to the larger expanses of the novel; but such aggrandisement was never something which interested Finlay. The poems he wrote, he told Derek Stanford in 1967, were intentionally reductive:

> One can do a lot by nuance, once one grasps the idea of working on a very small scale of effects. (. . .) But the trouble is that each poem has then its *own* set of rules, and you have to invent each poem from the start, which is rather hard.

One senses also in the poems an unburdening. In 'Straw' and 'The Estate-Hunters', the father is literally weighed down with the gear he decides he needs for the fishing trip, while the young soldier-artist in 'The Old Fisherman' becomes burdened with anxiety over the agreement he reaches with his drinking companion of the title. In the stories, such loads are made bearable by visions of beauty, by tenderness and friendship, and to a lesser extent by humour. However, the poems are able to offer situations in which the burden might be removed entirely: for example as 'Milk Bottles', of which at time of writing the poet has '159' but nonetheless can remember a time when he 'had none at all', and to which he can presumably return. But it is in the title poem that freeing oneself through a physical and social activity is conveyed most clearly:

> When I have talked for an hour I feel lousy
> – Not so when I have danced for an hour:
> The dancers inherit the party
> While the talkers wear themselves out and
>   sit in corners alone, and glower.

Images of transformation feature in the stories, most strikingly in 'The Boy and the Guess', with its imaginative riddling of a fishing boat as a pony, or a caravan. There is also a striking simile in a very early piece, 'Big House Grown Derelict' (printed in the *Glasgow Herald* in February 1952) which anticipates much of Finlay's later neo-classical work:

> And if, in fact, the house had been only a post-Victorian sham, then surely it was no worse to build private houses in the form of castles than to build, as we do, cathedrals in the form of aircraft hangars or banks in the form of the temples of the Greeks.

But these connections between disparate things are explored more fully in the poems, to the extent where one thing becomes or fuses into another, humourously in the case of 'Catch' with its 'helicapster' – a combined helicopter and lobster or, using the Orcadian term, 'lapster'. And when 'The English Colonel Explains an Orkney Boat', the most fitting object he can find to describe the fact that it has 'a point at both / Ends' is the lemon. This remains otherwise unexplored in *The Dancers*, but the equivalence of a northern boat to a Mediterranean fruit provides the seed for Finlay's later 'classicising' of Scottish sea-fishing and indeed of Scottish landscape, at Little Sparta.

Glasgow Beasts takes the notion of transformation further, with the poet becoming 'reincarnated' as a number of different beasts. The poems acknowledge their origin in work by the Japanese poet

Shimpei Kusano, so there is a playful Buddhist element to the changes. They belong also to a tradition of Scottish animal poems, which goes all the way back to Henrysoun's *Morall Faibillis*, with Edwin Morgan's version of Mayakovsky, 'A richt respeck for cuddies', and Norman MacCaig's frog and toad poems providing examples closer in time to *Glasgow Beasts*. MacCaig went through a kind of 'thaw' in the 1960s, departing from his earlier strictly formal, speculative work to more experientially based poems in free verse. Although MacCaig remained a close friend and supporter of MacDiarmid throughout this period, it's tempting to see Finlay, as writer, publisher and agitator, contributing to this thaw. At one level, the content of the individual poems is less important than the quick leaps from one type of animal to another – large and small, from different continents and of different species – but which are linked by the Glaswegian demotic in which they speak. A'' the poems are written in the past tense, emphasising the transitory nature of the 'lives' being described, and if the sequence opens with the fox's sense of freedom, and ends with the coal-horse's hard labour, there is less a sense of decline than of constant change. It's a striking shift from the rather static 'sadness' of the stories, a realisation of the self not in a sensitivity to unattainable beauty, but in playing out the transitory roles offered by the world, in moving through the transformations time affords.

In a letter of 1967 to Derek Stanford, Finlay wrote that:

> the real problem in every area is to try to formulate, not a 'wider' conception of reality (fascinating Man, profound Belsens, and all that Alvarez yugh!) but an idea of what a decent world might be.

This sentiment is very similar to that expressed in the much reprinted letter to Pierre Garnier of 17 September 1963, in which he describes the thinking behind his movement towards concrete poetry:

> . . . one does not want a glittering perfection which forgets that the world is, after all, also to be made by man into his

home. I should say . . . that 'concrete' by its very limitations offers a tangible image of goodness and sanity; it is very far from the now fashionable poetry of anguish and self. (. . .) It is a model of order, even if set in a space filled with doubt.

Finlay used that last sentence much later, in the course of his legal dispute with the French government over an awarded, and later revoked, commission for a work marking the bicentenary of the French Revolution. The words, 'a model of order, even if set in a space filled with doubt', initially referring to the need to make a home in the world, are rather chillingly printed on a card beneath the picture of a guillotine. The lack of acknowledged conflict in the early work stands in sharp contrast to the open conflict engaged in by Finlay in his life and work from the early 1960s onwards; flytings, the Little Spartan War, the conflict with the French authorities mentioned above, all of which he integrated into his work, which became themselves works of art, pieces of theatre. The point seems to be that in order to make a home in the world, to achieve 'goodness and sanity', one must be prepared to confront, to face down, one's enemies. Art does not exist meaningfully within the mind of the individual; it exists in the world, driving and focusing the relationships between people, whether friendships or enmities.

Another group of works from this period also link home with the guillotine, set gentleness next to terror. *Matisse chez Duplay* – realised in various forms, including a printed card, a neon text, and a mug – takes a text about Robespierre's simple rented room, and proposes it as an idyllic domestic scene by Matisse. 'The chamber of the deputy of Arras contained only a wooden bedstead, covered with blue damask ornamented with white flowers, a table, and four straw-bottomed chairs.' As in the earliest stories, no-one is present: it is an open question whether Robespierre is in his government chambers organising the execution of his enemies, or whether he himself has just been led away to the guillotine. The rural and domestic settings of the stories remain, but have been historicized; their relation to violence and destruction is made explicit. Such a dialogue between polarities can be linked to Finlay's early biography, with its emigration and impoverishment, and also to his experience of post-war Germany, whose hearths were literally in ruins. It becomes possible to articulate the latent conflicts and violence of the stories by understanding and presenting them within a much broader and deeper sense of history.

It is here that one sees Finlay's continuity of concerns most clearly, despite the changing forms he has used to make his work. Making a home in the world became meaningful to him not by continuing to produce texts which describe how one might do so, but by making an actual home which is also a work of art, and struggling to maintain its integrity against whatever threatened it. The later work is in the world, as sculpture, inscription, printed work, neon sign, and so on, so that the reader, conceived in the broadest sense, can understand them in terms of challenging and changing their own way of living in the world. The texts in this book are the early steps along the way to that realisation.

KEN COCKBURN

JUNE 2004

STORIES

Break for Tea

On a rainy July evening, on a barren grouse-moor, a fisherman was seated pipe-in-mouth against a rock. His oilskin cape was spread around him and made a shiny yellow pyramid. His legs clad in long black fishing-waders were extended on the grass. Nearby lay the heavy butt-end of his rain-globuled fishing rod from which descended loosely three trout flies of extraordinary hue. Smoke rose in little blue puffs from the man's pipe. Otherwise, he had a fossil-like appearance, his black and yellow surfaces turned stoically towards the moor.

Not far off – as a dragonfly flew – was a second fisherman. He, clad in a dark blue suit which the rain had dyed almost black, knelt in a reverent attitude before a camp fire whose ashes were enclosed within a circle of scorched stones. With long whistling exhalations of his Woodbine-scented breath he tried to coax a blink of crimson into the wet purple ash. When this had been done the reek rose up in clouds and the man drew back of a sudden with smarting eyes. Then, having piled onto the fire an armful of wet twigs, he set off to a nearby burn to fill two billycans.

The first fisherman now relinquished his seat by the rain-streaked boulder. Hampered by his cumbersome waders, he crossed to the point of the moor where the fire was burning as if passing from the sitting room to the kitchen of a house. Here, he took up a handy log and stirred the fire which flew up around him in a shower of sparks. Rain hissed on red-hot embers thus freshly exposed. Satisfied with the progress of the blaze, and especially with the good orange heart that was slowly forming in it, he flicked at a patch of wet turf with a spotted handkerchief, and sat down there on the windward side of the reek. As was evident, he was perfectly at his ease in the rent-free but rather bare lodgings afforded by the moor. He filled his pipe with lank worms of tobacco and shook out a newspaper which he presently began to read.

At length, as the fisherman sat peacefully by the camp fire under his imaginary mantlepiece, he was joined by his companion who laid the billycans down without a word. These, after some preparatory pokings, were propped carefully in the glowing heart of the blaze and left there till the burn-water they contained had begun to bubble. Whereupon a considerable quantity of tea was handspooned into both, and the resulting spate-coloured brew fished for and retrieved on the end of a branch. The two grey-wisped billys were left to cool awhile. Then, with contented lip-sucking noises, both fishermen drank.

Having sipped down with intense concentration as far as their tea-dregs, like little pieces of lukewarm water-logged twig, the two men briefly expectorated, and tapped their upended cans out on the grass. They settled themselves into new positions round the camp fire. When either coughed the rasping sound rose as if disembodied from the steam which wreathed around them thickly from their drying garments. The rain that had been merely a drizzle began to fall more heavily, and the mist slid down from the hills and across the moor till the two were presently shut alone in a little fire-lit slot. The tips of two fishing rods were hidden in the loose grey mist against which the backs of the fishermen seemed to find some support. Rain accumulated in the hollow of boulders, in ditches, in tins. It hissed on the red-flamed camp fire but could not put it out.

Anyone lost in that mist shortly afterwards might have heard with surprise a mouth-organ playing 'Home Sweet Home'. But the sound would likely have been drowned by the roaring of the rain, or confused with the sad bleating of the moorland sheep, or the many ditches that gurgled there, audibly brown.

The Blue-Coated Fishermen

A twelve year old boy, dressed to resemble his idea of a fisherman, was seated on the upper deck of a Glasgow tram. He wore wellington boots which he hoped would be taken for waders. In the lapel of his little green jacket was a large, brightly-coloured salmon fly. He held his fishing rod carefully between his knees while people clattered up and down the stairs of the swaying tram.

On the lower deck the tram was packed with shoppers going into the town. Upstairs, the passengers were mostly men on their way to the football match. Cigarette smoke greyed in the air, and the sunlight, striking through the spaces between the tenements, flickered across faces, raincoats and coloured scarves. The tram was full up, and four extra passengers were squeezed in the narrow space behind the seats at the back.

The tram moved with a choppy motion like a boat in a swell. It raced past all the stops, while now and then a man would swing aboard and duck in below the bar of the conductress's arm. The boy watched the platform in the tilted mirror on the stairs; and when he looked the other way he saw the oily hair of a standing passenger squeezed against the glass, leaving round dirty marks on it like a ball.

At the stop for the football ground the top deck emptied. Flags were fluttering bravely above the banked cinders of the terracing, and the crowd, moving round the top, were silhouetted against the sky. The tram's humming motor was shut off, and the boy heard the crowd cheer loudly as the home team ran out onto the field. There was a smaller cheer for the visiting team, and several incoherent shouts splashed up like slops. The men who had left the tram-car began to run. Swiftly they ran across the cinders, past the chewing gum sellers and the policeman riding erectly on his chestnut horse. There was yet a third cheer as the teams kicked off, and the boy had a vivid mental picture of the coloured jerseys, the green turf hacked around the goals, and the captain leaning forward over the clean, brown ball. For a moment he wished he had gone to the football match instead. He could have got in for only sixpence through the Boys' Gate.

The tram started off with a jerk, and the boy looked out at the shops – Ross's, Massey's and the Handy Stores. Outside the Troxy Picture House there was a long queue of children with here and there a mother with her young baby wrapped in a shawl. On the other side of the street, above a chalked wall, was the canal. Barges floated on the green water above the back windows of tenements, and several small boys were playing on the towpath. In the mirror, the boy saw the conductress making entries on a sheet of paper and pursing her lips when the tram shoogled her hand.

Suddenly the boy remembered that his fare had been overlooked in the rush. He thought he had better ask for a ticket in case an Inspector was to come aboard the tram. The next time the conductress came upstairs he held out his money, 'A penny half please.' With her red finger-nail she lifted the salmon-fly, admiring it.

'Gaun fishing, son?' she asked as she tore the ticket from the machine.

'Aye,' said the boy: and he looked in the glass of the window to see whether he had blushed.

'See and bring me a fush fir ma tea,' the conductress flung back as she clattered down the stairs.

The tram pointed its bow into open country and the boy kept watch for the Rail-Car at the side of the road. Presently, he caught sight of the rusted girders and the cigar-shaped carriage, but the tram went too quickly to allow him to have a good look. The conductress came back upstairs and began to reverse the seats for the return journey. She wound the handle to change the destination of the tram. 'Mind ma fush, noo,' she shouted to the boy as he jumped off the step. He waved his rod to her as if to say 'aye'.

The boy walked down the road between the New Houses, and into the more expensive avenue which led to the burn. He climbed the fence and crossed over the field with its straggly whin-bushes. The sun bored holes in the windows of the villas opposite, and he made his way to the deep pool where once a boy had been drowned. Two blue-suited fishermen were setting up their rods below the bridge, and he knew they would fish the pool first, and perhaps scare the trout. He hurried to set up his rod, his fingers shaking, his eyes roving eagerly over the rippled water. But suddenly a thin boy who was quite naked except for a pair of black drawers rushed out from the bushes and dived into the pool. He splashed about for a time, then climbed onto the bank and began to rub his tousled hair with a white towel. The blue-suited fishermen looked at the bather with disgust. Then they set off upstream, across the bridge.

The boy clasped his reel on the rod, drew the line through the hooks, and tied on the line the only fly-cast he had been able to afford. Making sure that the knot was tight, he hooked the cast in the handle of the rod and hurried on. The splashed water was still slapping the low banks of the bathing pool. A newly arrived fisherman came up to it, and kneeled back from the edge cunningly as he cast across. Two more fishermen arrived on bicycles, bending down to take the clips from their ankles before they wheeled their machines across the bridge. The boy hurried on hoping to find a free pool further upstream.

Now and then, as he walked, he caught sight of wadered fishermen, their rods flashing in the sun as they moved up behind the tree-trunks carved with initials and hearts. Boys carrying jam-jars and fishing-nets padded barefooted down the sun-warmed path. Sun-bathers wheeled their bicycles up the slopes of the hill, and newspapers and handkerchiefed heads showed above the grass. More boys were playing a game of football, the bladder rose up against the blue sky while there were shouts of 'Headers! Headers!' from the field below. Then the ball stotted down towards the boy's feet, and all the players patted their knees, 'To me, to me!' A groan went up as the fisherman mis-kicked the ball, and it flew away by the jackets laid down for goalposts.

The boy came to the old stone bridge, and he nipped through the hedge and down the bank. There were plopping rises of trout from below the bridge, and flies span down the water like miniature yachts. The boy prepared to cast, but just at that moment a little girl leaned over the parapet. 'Oh, mummy look at the fisherman,' she cried out delightedly. The trout ceased to rise, and the fisherman climbed despondently onto the path. He smiled to the little girl and her mother, then walked on.

Presently he found himself opposite the golf-course. Looking up through the trees he saw a plus-foured golfer steadying himself to drive. The clouted ball bounced down the slope and into the brackens and the golfer came down after it, looking all around. He walked to the wrong place and began to lift up the brackens with the head of his club. Then he scratched his head and threw down another ball.

As there was no one in sight, the boy climbed into the water to cast his fly. He looked at the overhanging trees and shortened his line. He cast, the line cracking like a whip, and the fly smacking down on the water with a splash. He was out of practice. He looked around to make sure no one was watching. Then he cast again with a slightly longer line. The fly hooked itself suddenly into the branch of a tree, and to retrieve it he had to wade out into midstream. The water poured in at once over the top of his wellingtons, but it soon grew warm in there with the heat from his toes. His casting improved as he waded upstream. Now and then he heard fishermen wading up behind him, but they always took to the bank and made off ahead. Once he rose a trout which stupidly missed the fly. He felt elated.

When he came out from the trees below the Refreshment Hut he saw that the sun had gone away. Drops of light like yellow syrup rolled slowly down the purple edges of the clouds. There was a roll of thunder in the distance, as if a heavy barrel was rolling around the edge of the sky. The air became blue and sticky. Rain fell, going on and off suddenly like a shower at the baths. There was a flash of yellow lightning and the boy blinked where he crouched against a rock. Then the storm passed, the boy's wet jacket steamed, and the salmon-fly's feathers stuck together like a lick of wet hair.

The clean water had soiled, and the boy searched under his lapel for a worm-hook. He began to turn over stones, looking for worms. Under every stone there were ants, and twisted white roots, but not a worm was to be seen in the dry soil. After a quarter of an hour the boy stood at the top of a long trail of overturned stones. He laid his free hand on his hip and stared back disconsolately. He wished he had bought worms in the tackle-dealers where the girl would count them like striped sweeties into your tin. Once he had made the breathe-holes in the tin too large. In the tram the worms had escaped and slithered wetly over the dry, dusty floorboards . . . He looked round and saw clouds of blue smoke uncurling between the trunks of the trees, and there by the camp-fire were the two blue-suited fishermen he had seen at the bridge. He thought they might lend him a few worms.

The fishermen were drumming-up. A billycan bubbled on the camp-fire. Their rods were propped against a tree; and their groundsheet, slung between two saplings, was pegged out by branches to make a shelter. On the top of the groundsheet was a puddle, causing it to sag. The fishermen were bent over the fire and one of them held a mustard-tin in which grains of sugar and leaves of tea were mixed up together. He emptied the mustard-tin carefully into the boiling water and gave the brew a stir round with a twig.

'See and mak' it taurry noo, Geordie,' the fisherman was saying. He looked round and saw the boy approaching the fire. 'Hulloa, son,' he shouted across, 'want a drink o tea?'

The boy came over shyly. 'I was wondering if you could lend me a few worms,' he said.

The tea-maker lifted the billycan aside on the end of a stick. The brew was darkening rapidly and was frothed on the top. 'Worms, son? Aye, sure. Hae ye goat a tun?'

'I can keep them in my pocket,' said the boy.

'Ach, ta, ta,' said the tea-maker, 'ye canna dae that.' He looked at the empty mustard-tin and handed it to the boy. 'Here, catch haud o that.' And he took from his pocket a tobacco-jar where worms were packed among wrappings of damp, green moss.

'Wull that dae ye?' he asked, taking out a wriggling handful. The boy nodded. 'Wait then noo an ye'll get a drink o tea.' The boy shifted awkwardly from one leg to the other, while the fisherman produced a tin mug and half-filled it from the can. 'It's guid taurry brew, that,' he said, winking. Then he squatted down on the grass and shared the billycan, sip about, with his pal. He patted the place beside him, 'Here, son, sit down and make yirsel' at hame.'

'Did ah hear ye say,' said the other fisherman, 'that ye'd caught nae fush?'

The boy blushed. 'I wasn't fishing very long,' he said. Then more brightly, he added, 'and the fish weren't biting because of the thunder.'

'Oh, aye,' said the first fisherman. 'If it hadna cam on thunder ye'd hae rooked the burn.' He looked at the salmon-fly on the boy's lapel. 'Yon's a smasher o' a flee that,' he said, smiling. 'Ah've aye wantit wan like that mysel.'

'Would you really like it?' asked the boy, beginning to unhook it. 'I've a bigger one than this in my drawer at home.'

'Naw, naw,' said the fisherman. 'Ah wis only kiddin. There's nae fush here tae match a flee like that.' He drew his creel over by the strap, and scattered his day's catch at his feet. There were a dozen little trout with shiny red spots which somehow made the boy think of wild strawberries. The fish were in good condition, fat and clean. The fisherman picked out six and began to thread them together on a length of string. They looked like coloured clothes pegs dangling on a line.

'Here,' he said, 'tak they hame tae yir mither. But dinna say ye catched them on that flee.' He jerked his head toward the salmonfly while the boy looked with delight at the little trout. 'Thank you very much,' he said. 'Could you please tell me what time it is now?' The fisherman took a large gold watch out of his waistcoat pocket, while an orange football-coupon envelope also emerged and fluttered to the ground. 'Five past five!' he said as he clicked back the lid. 'Oh,' said the boy, with disappointment, 'I'll have to go. I'll look out for you next week and I'll pay you back the worms.' 'Ach, never mind,' said the fisherman; and they both waved to the boy as he set off through the trees.

At the Refreshment Hut cyclists were sprawling on the grass with bottles of lemonade, and the shop-owner was flicking at flies with the end of a clout. The boy hurried by and kept a lookout for fishermen wading upstream. 'Got any?' he shouted down; and when the fishermen answered, or held up their fingers, he lifted up his own six trout on the end of the string. The fishermen would smile or shout up, 'My, that's grand!' He remembered the lost golf ball but it was too late; he had run past the place.

The bathing pool was empty now, and someone had left behind a towel which was hung over the whin-bushes to dry. Linked couples strolled across the bridge, and a flock of cyclists skimmed down the road. Their tyres hummed, their heads bent low over their dropped handlebars and their legs flashed round quickly in a pink blur. The boy wondered if it would be the same conductress on the tram.

A tram was standing in the terminus – a new one – and the green-coated driver was strolling up and down the grey, empty road. The seats on the top were facing different ways. The conductress came up to sort them but it was a different girl. The tram filled up and swayed off towards the town, and the boy forgot about the Rail-Car while he looked at the trout. When he next looked out of the window they were in Maryhill. There were long queues for the picture-houses, but now it was mostly couples who waited to get in. The tow-path by the canal was deserted. Over the top of the frosted windows of the pubs he could see bonneted heads, and hands holding pint glasses, while the circling fans cut the orange light into liths.

Presently, a man came and sat in the next seat, drawing away hurriedly when he felt the wet touch of the trout. He folded his clean Saturday raincoat in about him tightly, and worked his shaved chin in the folds of his white muffler. Feet clattered on the stairs. Young girls holding parcels of their dance shoes giggled and pretended to fall down as they passed through the tram. Snatches of talk about the football match made the boy lean over in his seat and prick up his ears. 'The gem wis a washout . . . The man wis offside . . . Ho, Malky, yir team wis doon the day.' Malky seemed to be the man who sat next to the boy. He eased his chin inside his muffler and shuffled his feet. 'Yon ref wants huntit off the perk.'

At Argyle Street, the boy left the tram and boarded a Red one. He looked out at the Art Galleries and at the circling froth on the Kelvin where it flowed between the factories, towards the Clyde. On the Partick railway-bridge a train was standing, its smoke blowing in white wisps into the street. There was scarcely anyone on the tram, though those crawling in the opposite direction were packed. The boy stickied the leather seat with his fish. 'Here,' said the conductor, 'take they offa that!' He rolled up the passage like a sailor, his cap thrust rakishly to the back of his head, his hand water-falling the piles of coppers in his pouch.

The boy alighted and set off up the street, swinging his fish. He clattered through the tenement close, and when he reached the top of the three flights of stairs he stood panting. He looked for the key behind the door but it was not there. He pulled the brass bell, and a light was switched on behind the glass, in the dark lobby. 'Here,' said his mother, 'you were to be in at five and it's gone seven. Your tea's in the oven, wasted. I told you last week you were to be in at the proper time.'

The boy clomped through to the kitchen and laid the fish nonchalantly on the varnished top of the coal-bunker. 'Losh,' said his mother, 'where did you get they?' She was so surprised she forgot to speak properly. The boy unhooked the salmon-fly from his lapel. 'I caught them of course,' he replied. 'Did you think someone gave them to me as a present?'

'Don't you be so cheeky,' said his mother. 'Take your tea out of the oven, and shift they fish away out of that.' She lifted a sheet of newspaper from below the cushion of the armchair. 'I'm away to set the fire for the morn. Your auntie's coming.' The door clicked behind her, and from the front room she shouted back, 'Shift those fish, now, sonnie, before you take your tea.'

The boy ducked under the white washing which hung on the pulley. He shifted the fish, then opened the oven door, taking out the plate that was balanced on the morning's kindles. He lifted the cosy from the pot and poured himself tea. It was poor, weak tea, he thought, not at all like the fishermen's. The tea-leaves were scattered thinly at the bottom of the pot, so he added several more spoonfuls and stood the pot on the gas. He stirred with the handle of a knife till the brew thickened and the leaves were like the leaves lying thickly in a dark autumn pool. He poured the weak stuff down the sink, and drank the new. Ah, that was the real thing – good tarry brew!

The Two Fishermen

The moor was raised hundreds of feet above sea level. It was cut off from the lower valley by its great height, like the topmost storey of a deserted warehouse only to be reached by a steep, twisting stair. This stair was the track which wound up to the moor by the side of a single-stranded waterfall of spectacular height. The track at its summit curved behind the waterfall which seemed then to close on it like a fairy door. The track had several times been climbed successfully by a jeep and once, unsuccessfully, by a lady in a limousine.

Up there stood a deserted dwelling. Rain was hosing down its mossy slates in a thin grey stream. It tapped among the tall, bent nettles by the weatherbeaten door. It smote with a solid sound on the cracked doorstep. In a holed bucket it made a sound like a lapping hare. It cat-hissed on the red ashes in the hearth within the house.

Two fishermen had come to poach on the private grouse-moor. Rain had fallen. Throwing capes about their heads and shoulders they had stumbled across the moor to shelter in the empty house. The door stood ajar. They entered the kitchen.

From the rotted plaster walls they took lathes to light a fire. They cooked their stolen trout, the size of clothes-pegs. They brewed tea in their billycans. They drank contentedly, their bottoms on the stone flags, their backs supported by a rough wooden bench scarred here and there by axe blows that had glanced off. Their feet in stocking soles were placed near the fire to dry, causing wisps of steam like pale feathers to rise from their socks. The rain's sound drove them into the silence like long grey skelfs.

One fisherman was a tall thin fellow. While his shoulders hunched upwards against the sound of the rain, his soiled suit hung in damp cavernous folds. Into one such cranny had crept a moth which looked out with pale, prehistoric eyes. On the man's moist brow the reflected firelight showed like a watery sunset. His sparse moustache bristles were like the bones of little trout.

The second fisherman was small and plump. He was clad in an unbuttoned battledress. His lips were shaped pertly around a soundless whistle. His toes of a tobacco-colour emerged from his many-holed socks. His hair, above his pink brow, was sleeked and shiny with brilliantine or rain. Sometimes he jerked his eyes toward the window where their merriment was momentarily doused in the opaque stream.

The fishermen, while waiting for the rain to abate, had made themselves at home. Their empty billycans, on the uneven flags, leaned sideways with a suggestion of tipsy sentimentality. On the door hung a limp sou'wester, animated now and then by a fierce draught.

Two fishing rods lay lengthwise across the mantlepiece. In the corner, since the two men had come for the weekend, were piles of waterproof bedding folded neatly back.

The taller fisherman looked at the frying-pan which stood improperly on the sheet of newspaper that had served as a breakfast cloth. He lifted the pan into the hearth, and searched in his pocket for a handkerchief which he presently withdrew. With the air of a waiter in an expensive hotel, he harried a few soot-crumbs from the newspaper to the floor. Racing results, like messages in a curious code, were then revealed. He cleared the tablecloth entirely and began to read it.

The plump fisherman produced a small green packet of cigarettes. He drew forth a slender butt-end which the rain had soiled, and thrust it into the aperture of his whistling lips. He turned it several times like a screw till it fitted perfectly. A match was struck, and sheltered in a cup of hands as if in a gale.

The taller fisherman laid down his newspaper and looked across the hearth towards his pal. He fixed his eyes on a battle-blouse pocket which bulged. He coughed once or twice, as if to clear a hole in the silence, like ice, before he spoke.

'Gie us a tune, Jock,' he asked in wheedling tones.

The smaller fisherman blew a smoke-puff shaped like a pigeon.

'Och, no the noo.'

'Och go on . . . a wee tune . . . to cheer us up.'

The plump fisherman nicked his butt-end and took out his mouth-organ. He blew a few trial scales which proved the notes to be clogged. He tapped the instrument on his heel, and blew again. The taller fisherman closed his eyes with a blissful expression, and called across the hearth for favourite tunes. He sang the lyrics in a hoarse, lugubrious voice, the vowel-sounds being drawled out thinly like the hooting of owls.

'Come and sit by my side if you love me
Do not hasten to bid me adieu
I'll be here in the Red River valley
I'll be waiting my darling for you . . . oo . . . oooo.'

A footstep fell heavily on the flags by the door; and the tune, and its vocal accompaniment, were broken off. Both fishermen glanced round nervously. They were struck dumb by a sudden recollection of their poaching.

A man of amazing proportions thrust into the room. He was clad in tweed clothes of aristocratic cut. His blue eyes, in his red, healthy face, shot out keen glances like chromium grappling hooks. His eyebrows, coloured like an eagle's feathers, were thickly tufted. Two dogs, of a breed which suggested a cross between a collie and husky, detached themselves from his heels, slinking away into corners where they growled. An instant later a third dog pranced into the kitchen, and ran round twice as if acknowledging applause. It shook its wet coat thoroughly, then vanished through the door.

The shepherd crossed to the bench and sat down, his enormous presence looming heavily over the two fishermen. He spoke in loud hearty tones. 'You're here then!' he said. 'A terrible day . . . terrible althegether . . .' The fishermen made no reply. They stared into the hearth where pools of muddy water were gathering round the shepherd's massive boots. They were almost certain they had been caught red-handed by the laird.

The plump fisherman then had an idea of astonishing brilliance.

He would test the man's identity with his fags, using the small, green packet as a kind of litmus paper. If the man was the laird he would refuse the cheaper brand. He would doubtless have his own expensive brand of smokes. For a moment the fisherman was uplifted by the thought of his own brilliance. He drew out the Woodbine packet and opened the flap.

'Smoke?'

'No, no,' said the tweed-clothed stranger, waving it away. 'I can't be doing with those wee smokes at all. I've the pipe here in my pocket, thanks all the same.' He took out the pipe and began to fill it slowly, prodding down the tobacco with his thumb. The smaller fisherman was horrified with his experiment. He took a fag in his shaky fingers, and lit it with a slow, desperate calm. Then the shepherd did something that put both fishermen at ease. He leaned forward and spat into the embers of the fire. The spit briefly sizzled. The fishermen relaxed. They shifted their limbs, and exchanged a broad wink across the hearth. The shepherd put a match to his pipe, and addressed the pale town-faces uplifted to his.

'Did you hear,' he began, 'that the Hydro-Electricity Boys are making the whole glen into a loch? Yon paint sploshes on the rock down yonder will be the head of the dam. When they get it built the water will be over this house.' He spread his huge hand above the flags and raised it slowly to suggest the rising water. 'There'll be more trouts' nests in the chimney there than there are swallows' nests now!' As he spoke the shepherd's blue eyes twinkled above the bowl of his pipe. In his imagination, developed strongly in the solitude of the hill, he saw the kitchen tenanted by the grey, gliding shapes of many trout. Quickly he turned to see the effect of his speech on the two fishermen.

At the mention of the trouts' nests the two fishermen had gazed at each other pityingly. They began to semaphore across the hearth with broad winks, inspired partly by lofty pity for the shepherd's ignorance, and partly by a desire to forget that they had taken him for the laird. The shepherd observed the winks and quietly decided to revenge himself in due course. He was in no immediate hurry as he was eager to talk. He had a fund of anecdote, amounting to a kind of personal mythology, which he was pleased to impart. He was a man of lively intelligence and a strong sense of humour.

The fishermen feigned to listen to the shepherd's tales. But their thoughts centred on fishing – seconds that were running to waste. They had no wish to be soaked through twice in a single weekend. Yet the delay was irksome to anglers as keen as they. They strained their ears, listening to the rain that had slightly abated, pattering down with small dark sounds like innumerable, whirling, used leaves of tea. The collies sat quietly in their corners, licking up their rain-matted coats into quick-drying spikes. The third dog entered, unobserved, and made off with a loaf of bread which it chewed beyond the door.

The shepherd moved from tale to tale with extraordinary exuberance. The connection between each story was slender, like a broken paper clip holding together miscellaneous documents. He paused now and then to hold a match to his pipe.

'There was a wee Englishman was brought to Meggurnie to shoot the foxes. Damn the fox the man had ever seen! So they had a collection in the district to get the wee fellow his fare down South. He was just going away in the bus when he stood up all of a sudden shouting. 'There's a fox! There's a fox!' And he went and shot off the conductor's hat . . .! What do you make of that now?' the shepherd asked.

The taller fisherman considered the story with suspicion. He tried to picture a fox but all he could think of was a greyhound which his imagination deftly coloured red. If the man had aimed his gun at the fox how had he happened to shoot off the conductor's hat? The man must have been a very poor shot indeed. Or else . . . it suddenly became clear to the fisherman that the tweed-clothed countryman was having him on. He winked violently at his pal. They asserted their superiority by several broad winks. There was no putting it over two town boys smart as they!

The shepherd skipped straight on to another tale. This time the two fishermen were on their guard. Their eyes exchanged narrow, hostile glances. They listened for the sound of the rain which appeared to have gone off. 'There was a fox came to Meggurnie once. It was coming on lambing-time . . .'

The smaller fisherman yawned. He looked at the shepherd cheekily, while he winked at his pal so often that smoke from the dead fire seemed to have blown into his eyes.

The shepherd stood up abruptly, abandoning his tale. His foot caught the two billycans and set them rolling to and fro on the uneven flags. He put his hand to his ear dramatically. 'What's that?' he said. He crossed to the window and stared out, the fishermen staring after him, their earlier apprehensions renewed.

Two rabbits were playing leap-frog on the moorland track. A ewe cropped the grass, its face glistening in the faint smir of rain. The wet grass-heads shone like mist. There was nothing else to be seen.

At length the shepherd turned to face the fishermen, and wiped his brow heavily though it was quite dry. 'I thought I heard the laird's jeep,' he said excitedly. 'Did you not think yourselves you heard a car?' His blue eyes twinkled brightly but were hidden by his sleeve.

'What like a man is the laird?' asked the taller fisherman.

'Terrible,' said the shepherd, flatly. 'He's the fiercest man I ever met in my life. I mind the day he got a boy fishing just down yonder . . .' He broke off, leaving the fearful consequences in doubt . . .

'Will the laird be around the day?' put in the plump fisherman.

'Like as not,' said the shepherd nonchalantly. 'I wouldn't be surprised if the man were to walk in now . . .' He looked over his shoulder, suddenly, towards the door. The taller fisherman sprang up and began to dismantle his fishing rod, stuffing the parts hurriedly into their canvas case, and finding strange difficulties with loops and knots.

Just at that moment, a patch of sunlight, like a slab of margarine appeared on the flags. It wavered once or twice then thickened, till it spread like farm butter across the floor. It yellowed on the shepherd's boots and seemed to remind him that his dinner-time was drawing near. 'Well,' he said, 'I'll be holding away on down the road. I'll not be keeping you here when you're wanting down to the burn to fish.' He crossed to the door and stuck his head out momentarily into the sunshine. 'Just the very day for the trouts, the very day . . .' He waved, and was gone in a rush of dogs which leaped to his heels.

The two fishermen began to pack at once. Neither spoke. Sometimes they halted to listen for the sound of a car. There was no sound save the poignant roaring of the swollen burn. They packed at an amazing speed. They stepped into the sunshine tentatively, like two paddlers walking on a beach where there is much broken glass. They regretted their slim, incriminating fishing rods. They halted for a moment to disguise the rods, tying on bunches of the moor's wet heather. Then they set off swiftly down the track, by the side of the falls.

The shepherd stepped back silently into the wet shadow of the wood. The two collies sat at his heels. The third dog was gripped tightly by the shepherd's fist to prevent it bounding out after the two men. The fishermen came into sight, and the shepherd observed the way in which they glanced all round. His eyes twinkled like two large raindrops in the shadow. He was already considering a tale which began, 'There were two fishermen came to Meggurnie. They were boys from the town . . .' He embroidered the tale, and improved it considerably, as he held on down the road with his dogs at his heels.

Fisher by the Stove

One day the other August I was writing in my cottage kitchen that was grey with smoke leaking out from the stove. I was drinking black tea that had been stewing since breakfast time, while the clock showed it was the middle of the afternoon. The tea had left red rings round the inside of the white cup at several levels at which I had left it to stand between sips.

The stove is a great hulk of a thing. Once it was painted green all over but now it is mostly brown with rust and black with soot. I can still read its name, 'The Duchess', with the tip of my finger. It gives almost no heat but a lot of smoke which is meant to go up a pipe in at the back. When I come downstairs in the morning to light the stove, I always look for the grass or barnacles that are sure to take root, sometime, on the top of it. In damp weather I look for barnacles and in the summer for grass.

The smoke, this day, drove me to the door with a choking sensation. I stood on the front step looking out at the mist. It must have been raining, and the fence wires wore raindrops like glass marbles while my seven hens looked bedraggled and fed-up. They stood a little way off, sunk in the mist, making low, sad noises like the foghorns of lost ships out at sea.

Suddenly I heard the thud of a man's footsteps on the wet ground, and a moment later a little man clothed in black strode by the house. He carried a fishing-rod, and a khaki haversack hung from his shoulder and bounced on his hip as he walked along. On his head was a bonnet which he did not seem to wear, but carried like a native-bearer carrying a rock with no hands.

A cigarette, which I guessed was damp, stuck out from his lip.

Grey smoke curled from it, and wreathed around his shoulders as if he had brought his own mist with him down from the hill. He looked a lonely man, like a character out of Wordsworth, but he came from Glasgow as it turned out. His suit was not really black but was only wet through, and it came back to a bright blue colour while he sat in a chair, to dry, in front of my stove.

I filled the stove with as many dry logs as it would hold. Then I roared it to make a good heat. As always happens, the stove grew red-hot in a few isolated places, and buckled up, causing the kettle and teapot to slant alarmingly. At the same time it made noises like a fierce animal. Most of the heat went up the chimney but enough came our way to make the fisher steam.

The fisher vanished in a cloud of white steam. I handed him in a cup of fresh tea, and listened to his low, deep, husky, disembodied voice. He told me he had fallen into the burn, but his sudden plunge from a stone, into cold, rushing water did not seem to have worried him in the least. All that worried him was the loss of his catch that had floated away through the mouth of his haversack, the flap being open.

He came back slowly, out of the steam. Here, I saw a patch of unshaven chin; there, was a length of his suit, now bright blue. He still had his bonnet balanced on the top of his head, a few flies stuck in it, like real flies resting on the side of a rock. I asked if I might see the flies and he took off his bonnet to show them to me. His hair was thinning and was brushed back carefully, in strands.

We talked about wet-fly fishing, and then about worm-fishing, in the little burns like the one he had come from, up in the hill. I knew without having asked that neither of us had ever fished the dry-fly. He told me he went out fishing every weekend, and I thought of his long, lonely fishing-shifts, worked each weekend between the close of March and the start of October. On weekdays he worked in a factory, stoking a furnace, he said.

While we talked and drank tea I looked at his suit. It was a fifty-shilling suit, but the way he wore it it looked just right for the hill. Even more than a fine tweed suit I could see it blending with the rocks and brackens. Perhaps the weather had softened it as it had done his khaki haversack, which would not have looked out of place in my shed, hanging beside the rabbit-snares I never use but like to look at because of their shapes. The khaki haversack, an old gas-mask container, looked a whole world away from poison gas. It was part of the world of sad rain, fishers, and spates that sound like a drunk, husky Irishman singing 'Galway Bay'.

The fisher took out his pocketbook and began to show me fly-casts. I made the mistake of saying I liked one, and immediately he took it out and insisted that I have it. I tried to make him take one of my own fly-casts in exchange, but he would not. I felt I could not show him my own casts because several of them were in a fankle, whereas his were all neatly rolled, with obvious care.

I showed him a minnow I had made from a tin, more for fun than for fishing with: and he showed me several flies he had tied himself. They were small, dark flies. My minnow was too big, and I had not been able to resist the temptation of painting it up in bright, useless colours. It looked like a model of a man-eating shark. The fisher squinted at it, but said nothing as he laid it back in my hand. Minnows with black dots and white molars were not for him.

I thought of W.B. Yeats's peasant-fisherman, the grey Conne-mara man who went at dawn, alone, to drop his fly beside a dripping stone. Yeats said, in almost the next line, that he was 'but a dream'. My friend was no dream: and I thought of the two, the grey one from his squat cabin and the dark one from his Glasgow tenement, tall as a cliff. I thought that if they ever met on the high-tops in the soft fine rain, by the red and white water rushing down the stones, they would have something in common and would speak for a while.

I remembered one March night when it was bitterly cold, and I was going round the side of the loch in the bus. The tops of the hills were still under snow, and they floated above the dark loch like huge, pale stars. The loch was like a cold, dark slate. All the same, the Glasgow fishers were out for the start of the season, and I could see a dozen bonfires on the far shore. When the breeze blew the fires brightened like the lit end of a cigarette when the smoker takes a draw.

Afterwards the lochside pub was packed with fishers, little men in blue suits holding frothed brown pints, all talking at the tops of their voices, shooting their hands out sideways to sketch in trout. The bar was tiny; and the floor, and the half-dozen tables, were a clutter of rods and haversacks and creels. All the fishers were clad in the same way as my friend by the stove, now almost dried out.

I looked across to the windows, filled with clouds and wet sheep and one hen that perched there to pick the whitewash, beyond the dark pane. It was about seven o'clock, but already the light was fading, or it was preparing to rain down in buckets. My friend said he would have to go and catch a bus. I had wood to collect for the stove, so I offered to walk down the path with him part of the way. He swung his haversack over his shoulder and grinned wryly at the light feel it had. A dozen or fifteen small trout can make quite a weight on one's shoulder. His would be floating down towards the far sea.

The mist was still white among the pine-tops. It wreathed among the dark needles in long, thin strands like strips of wet tissue paper. We went down the path, through the wood, the fisher in front till he lost the thin path among the tall brackens. I went in front, then, to show the way. We came to the gate down at the dyke and there we halted. There were dripping sounds from inside the wet wood.

I opened the gate. This was where I stopped to gather my night's supply of logs. I said to the fisher that he must knock at my door if he came by again. Even as I said it, I knew he would not. I knew that next week he would be far up some other little burn, within a bus-ride from Glasgow, but still remote. I thought I saw him climbing upwards over slippery boulders, through the fine rain, till at the last fall he would step to the bank and brew a can of tea. I saw him crouched under rainy clouds by his blaze, perhaps frying a few of his little trout, before taking down his fishing-rod.

We said goodbye, and when he had almost vanished in the mist he turned and waved. I waved back: and then I stepped down into the brackens to search for logs. In no time my trousers were soaked through, and I saw my wet jacket glistening out of the corner of my eye. I dived my hand down in the brackens, feeling for logs. It was like guddling for them. They were wet, cold and slippery to lift. I thought of the fisher all the time as I walked back to the house, carrying the heavy logs balanced on my hip.

I laid the logs down by the block, in front of the house, and split them with blows of the axe into foot lengths. Carrying an armful of logs, I pushed open the kitchen door and went in. I stacked the logs to dry on the side of the stove. Three armfuls is usually enough to keep the stove burning for half a day.

The fisher's chair was still standing in by the stove, with a round pool of water in below. I stared at what was left behind on the chair itself, and I was scarcely willing to believe my eyes. I dropped the pile of logs with a clatter down in the hearth and picked up the small trout by the tail. How it had got there was a mystery. Had it swum inside the fisher's clothes when he fell in the water? Was it one of his own catch? I could only guess. I looked at the trout with astonishment as I held it in my hand.

Presently I took the trout through to the sink and slit it up with the kitchen knife. Then, while I dusted the trout with oatmeal, I set the pan on the top of the stove to heat. When a curl of blue smoke was rising from it I let the trout down gently in the sizzling fat. Being fresh, it curled up at once, and the fat sizzled like a cloudburst. I stared at the frying trout, which was more of a mystery than any other trout that had been in the house before.

Boy with Wheel

I was walking home from the village one evening when I saw the boy ahead of me in the road. At first I thought he was alone but when I caught up with him a few minutes later I saw he had company of an unusual kind. He had brought along his bicycle wheel to keep him company on his long walk home from the village with his mother's messages.

It was just growing slightly dark. Owls were hooting in the brown fir-woods on the one side of the road; and bats, those nocturnal swallows, were swerving and diving above my head. On the other side of the road, beyond the sharp dyke, the fields were filling up with blue dusk. It seemed to be trickling out of the woods like smoke from a wet or dying blaze.

All the gates to the fields stood wide open. The cattle were in byres. The open gates, leaning slightly inwards, made me think of ghost-cattle slouching in between the posts. I seemed to see the lowered heads and swinging udders, and even to hear the tapping of the drover's stick on their flanks.

As I hurried to catch up on the boy, there was no real sound save my own clattering footsteps. The silence was as if the strath had been wrapped in ten thousand reams of tissue paper. Now the sun had set the air had turned chilly. The road, with the dark woods on one side of it, seemed to catch all the light there was and it shone like dull metal.

The boy had heard me coming and stood in at the road's edge holding his bicycle wheel. I knew him quite well. He stayed about a mile farther down the road in my own direction. His father was dead. His mother nearly always wore a dark, cloth mourning-coat when she came on the bus. I was surprised each time I saw her clutch a straw shopping-basket instead of a bunch of flowers in her pale, ringed hand.

As I came up on the boy he gave the wheel a little shove that set it spinning smoothly on the road ahead of him. It was an ordinary silver-coloured bicycle wheel, rusted in a few places but with all its spokes seemingly intact. He had it gripped on the end of a few feet of fence-wire that secured it but did not interfere with its running. The wheel was, in a way, like a dog on a rope. There was no tyre on it, of course.

The boy himself was about thirteen years of age. On his head, instead of a cap, he wore one of those leather helmets and the earflaps were unbuttoned. His grey, thick jersey, I guessed, had been knitted for him by his mother. His boots were as clattery as my own, studded with heavy nails.

While the wheel span ahead of us, on the crown of the road, I could not help staring at it fixedly. If I raised my eyes for a second I had an urge to return them to the wheel at once. In its silver shape I lost my thoughts as easily as in a starry sky on a frosty night. The tiny sound span off the rim like an endless audible inch-tape that glittered in my ears. Though my footsteps measured yards on the solid road, the wheel made me lose almost all sense of space as long as I stared at it. When I looked up we were already half-way to the end of the fir-woods. We had covered half a mile in silence, and as if in an instant or so. The boy, too, was staring fixedly at the wheel, and listening to the bright, hypnotic sound spinning off the rim of it, as it went along.

Then suddenly we hit a bad patch on the road. There were puddles right across the road from side to side. Though the puddles were dry, they were filled to the brim with shadows that made them stand out plainly on the pale surface. The rim lost its steady sound and began to scrunch, while each time the wheel hit a puddle it made a violent turn and sometimes lost so much momentum it toppled over.

The boy persevered with the wheel. He probably felt it would have been cheating to carry it over the bad patch. He let it drag him about the road like a big, wild dog. Sometimes it dashed over towards the dyke as if to sniff for rabbits. Then it would head for the grass bank below the dark woods. Once or twice it turned right around and made back towards the village, with the boy hurrying along behind and vainly trying to head it off. He grinned at me as if apologising for his stubborn pal – the bicycle wheel.

By this time it was almost dark. When the wheel was running smoothly again, the boy's thoughts began for the first time to skip away ahead of it. They skipped ahead to his supper. I knew what he was thinking because he suddenly looked sideways at me and said: 'Will she have your supper ready when you get in?'

'She' was my wife. I was not quite sure what I ought to reply. 'I hope so,' I said. 'How about you?'

I thought of his mother with her black cloth coat and weary expression. The boy had several brothers – little ones as well as big ones who were old enough to work. I vaguely supposed his mother had a difficult life.

'Oh, she'll have my supper ready,' he said at once.

There was more than a trace of boyish boasting in the way he spoke. I stared at the wheel in silence. In the silver blur of it I lost my picture of the dark mother in the lamplit room. As from afar, I heard him say: 'If she doesn't have my tea ready you'll hear me swear.'

A car came down the strath and we had to step to the edge of the road for a second to let it go by. On its four rubber-shod wheels it ran luxuriously. I looked at our wheel with fresh eyes. I listened to it spinning. It was as if we had the first wheel of all, the archetypal wheel; and I thought of wooden wheels, whips cracking, slit-eyed folk clad in furs. Our steps came clattering behind the wheel with an awkward sound as we started down a slope and it set the pace for us.

At length we reached the end of the fir-woods where the boy turned off. His yellow window was set in the thick darkness below the tall bank with the trees on it. The short road down to the house was spread with gravel, but just as the wheel began to scrunch he lifted it up and tucked it in below his arm. His shadowy figure turned and waved to me, then he started to run the rest of the way to the house. His big steps took him as if from stepping-stone to stepping-stone, as he leaped the ruts in the road. A dog started barking in a shed somewhere at the back of the house.

Just as he entered the backyard I saw him swing up the wheel on the end of the fence wire. The air whistled in the spokes. He birled it once or twice round his head, and when he let it go it rose at a steep slant and hit the top of the bank. That was where the house had its rubbish pit. I heard the wheel strike on what was probably an old rusted kettle or a basin in the pit. Simultaneously, or an instant after, the back door of the house was banged shut.

The Sea-Bed

Two blue-jersied, brown-legged boys were fishing with penny handlines from the rocks.

The rocks there ran right out into deep water. There were several lines of rocks, parallel to each other like the platforms of a railway station, with the deep blue, calm sea between.

The two boys had naturally gone to fish on the very tip of the rocks that were furthest out into the sea. They were about 500 yards out from the black cliffs that curved round and sheltered them from the breeze blowing beyond the bay. On the top of the cliffs were a few whitewashed houses with blue roofs.

On the other side of the rocks, to the right, was a sandy shore with some tethered boats on it, and one rotted boat, half-sunk in the sand like an enormous footstep. Fishing-nets, brown triangles between slanted posts, stood further along the shore.

There was not a ripple on the top of the water, inside the bay. The boys' lines went down at a slant into the deep water, and the baits could be seen clearly as they rested near the sandy bottom. The bottom was not all sandy but the sand showed in small yellow patches between the brown and purple seaweed, shiny and strong, and some of it like straps of liquorice.

Both boys had removed their boots and thick woollen stockings. They were careful not to cut their feet on the smashed shells of the mussels they used for bait. It was the best bait they knew of. The mussels were stored in two identical, rusted syrup-tins, and they had a strong smell as they were no longer fresh.

A strong, clean, salt smell rose from the sea, and that and the smell of the mussels made the wholesome yet mysterious smell of fishing the boys loved.

So far they had caught nothing; but dozens of small, black fish, scarcely larger than minnows swam round the baits. They bit at the soft mussels fiercely, and swam away with little pale fragments of them in their dark mouths. They came back for more as soon as they had done.

The mussels broke into pieces rapidly before the fierce bites. But the fish were too tiny to get their mouths round the large sea-hooks, rusted and thick-gutted, on which the bait was impaled. The boys had to open more mussels, and draw up their lines to re-bait them every few minutes.

Now and then, one of the boys gave a terrific jerk to his line so that the heavy lead sinker was dragged up from the sand. The sinker came up like a weapon through the shoal of fish that fled in all directions, leaving the water empty. Then, the sinker was let to drop back, and sand rose up in small yellow puffs. By the time these had settled the fish had come back to steal the bait.

The boys were not bored in the least though they were not catching anything. It was fascinating to put fresh mussels on the hook, and to watch the small fish swing them like punch-balls from side to side till they fell apart. And it was nice to be together down there on the rocks, barefooted and with rolled-up sleeves, within smell of the sea.

The two boys had been watching their baits intently for more than an hour and there was now a confusion in their minds as to the size of the small fish.

When they first came down the cliff-path, and made their way carefully across the seaweed-slipperied rocks, they had spoken of catching rock-cod, and other fish of a size they indicated by holding their hands two feet apart. The two-feet fish were almost a certainty and when it was a question of luck, they held their hands out even wider, and talked excitedly, hearing the seaweed go pop below their boots like exclamations of surprise.

But now they had forgotten all about this. They had put ounce instead of pound weights on the imaginary scales on which they weighed their catch. And their catch was still swimming round in the deep water below.

It was now five o'clock in the evening and the tide was supposed to be on the turn somewhere about that time.

And presently, there was a strange, almost imperceptible movement of the calm sea. It was not a movement that you could see exactly, it was more of a movement you could feel. And a little wave rose up and slapped the rock on which the boys were kneeling, wetting the bare knees of the boy who was closest to the edge. He drew back instinctively but there were no more waves.

Despite the breeze blowing outside the bay, the sea was calm to the very edge of the sky. There, a small, poignant sail crept slowly along. It was a brown sail, a smack's sail – perhaps the sail of one of the boys' fathers' boats.

The tide began to rise up the rocks. The boys moved back to the next rock, a little nearer to the cliffs, and in time the water thinly covered the smashed shells they had left behind. The white shells shone through the water that was too thin as yet to be blue.

Now the lead sinkers rested on a new patch of yellow sand. It was just like the previous patch but the small, black fish had gone away, so there was an air of Sunday, almost, about the empty water. The mussels hung quite still above the yellow sand. Even so, neither of the boys was in the least discontented. They watched the baits. They looked down their slanting lines, turned around their brown wrists once or twice for safety's sake

Suddenly, about an hour later, one of the boys felt that his skin no longer fitted him. His heart stopped beating for a second as he watched the great cod.

He knew it was certainly a cod because of the dark tuft that sprouted from its chin. He knew, also, that the tuft was not really dark, but was only dark like the rest of the fish above the yellow sand, with the light coming down on it from above.

The cod swam up to the bait and sniffed it without touching it. Then it turned and swam quickly out to sea. It was gone like the shadow of a bird, quickly, soundlessly. The boy let out his breath which he had been holding all the time without meaning to.

The boy let out his breath and stared at the sea-bed. It was just the same as before, but now it had an air of silence and emptyness which was not like Sunday. It had been changed by the cod.

The boy found himself shivering, and his hand was making bites at his end of the line, so that the sunk mussel was twitching and shivering too. His excitement ran down his fingers and down the line to the bait like lightning running down a wire and into the ground. It was several minutes before he stopped shivering violently.

The fact was, he could scarcely believe in the cod which had come like a herald from the sea-depths, for such a short space of time. He stared downwards, rubbing his finger on his lip, thinking, wondering. Then suddenly the sea-bed down there became real to him, and he could feel it going out and out, below the sea, further down than even it was there, and frightening to think of. He looked inland towards the cliffs.

For a long while he looked at the path going up the cliffs, and at the whitewashed houses catching the bright, clear light that came off the sea. Gulls were hovering and diving above the blue roofs. The windows caught the light as if the glass of them was water. He could see an old man walking along the top of the cliffs.

After a time, he looked back down to his friend, a few yards from him. When he spoke he tried to make his voice sound ordinary, because his friend had an ordinary look as he squatted on the rocks' edge, staring down his line. His voice came out low, and trembling slightly.

'Geordie, I saw a muckle cod. It cam tae my line.'

The other boy raised his head for a second and looked across without much interest and probably with the idea that his friend was imagining things. He knew his friend had a strong imagination.

'How did ye no catch it?' he said, and he looked back at his line.

The boy who had seen the cod did not answer this question. He was not very concerned about not catching the cod, though it now struck him that it would have been rather frightening if he *had* hooked it. He stared down into the water which was near and at the same time a long way away.

There was silence between the two boys for a long stretch of time. The light began to fade just a little, and shadows filled the holes in the rocks and cliffs. The boys moved further back along the line of rocks, and kept an eye on the tide.

The sail of the smack was much nearer – a big, red-brown sail made of rough canvas, so visibly rough that one of the boys felt an itch to touch it, in the ball of his thumb. Nets were hung to dry from the mast, and the corks made dotted lines that were also nice to look at, against the blue sky. The hull of the boat was painted a dark blue that looked black.

The boat rose and fell gently, and the boy whose thumb had been itching felt a similar itch bother him in the soles of his feet. He felt the black rocks, very solid and unmoving below his bare feet. And at the same time he felt the hollow planks of the boat going up and down the waves. He felt the boat going along lightly and containing its own air inside its dark hold.

An hour or more passed. The boys had moved in much further towards the cliffs. Now the one who had not seen the cod had a flounder and a small dog-fish laid beside his can of bait. The flounder flapped at intervals and the boy then gave it a good clout against the rock. But it had several spasms of cold, wet flapping before it lay finally still.

The boy who had seen the cod, but who had caught nothing, was not in the least envious of his friend's catch. He did not feel envious because of course he had the idea of the cod's great size inside his head, and he could not help measuring his friend's catch now and then, with his eye, in a superior way. But his friend had his own standards and was delighted with his catch.

The boy who had seen the cod looked at his line going down into the water, very deep and dark, but still transparent as it had been all along. He wrestled with sensations that in his twelve years of life, in a fishing family, in a small town he had not hitherto experienced. He tried to sort them out methodically, in the way he sorted out his fishing line when it got in a fankle.

When the boy had loosened the several sensations of the cod, the deep, dark water, and the sea-bed going out and out in below the sea, he tried to turn the sensations into thoughts. This he found difficult. He went on puzzling and staring at his line, while his friend caught another small flounder, about the size of an envelope, and another tiny one about the size of a stamp.

He himself got no bites, and he was quite glad to stare at the water merely, and think. Every now and then they lifted boots and stockings and bait-tins and moved down the rocks.

Dusk fell across the sea. The sail, now, had vanished in behind the cliffs. The breeze changed its direction, and began to blow, suddenly, into the bay. It was pleasant to think of the boat tied up in the harbour, behind the cliffs.

The breeze struck the water in different places and there it went goosefleshed and suddenly black. The gooseflesh became constant so that the baits were no longer to be seen. The boy who had seen the cod rolled down the sleeves of his thick jersey, and felt the warm wool clothe his wrists in a way that was comforting. Slowly, he began to put on his stockings and his boots, so that he had a less intimate contact with the rocks, through the thick soles. That, too, was what he wanted, after puzzling for a long time about the cod.

Suddenly, because he felt his friend's weight still planted without reticence on his bare ankles, as he felt down through his line for more bites, he stood up on his feet with an almost violent movement. He began to wind his line up from the bed of the sea. As the wet section of it reached his fingers, he shivered. He laid the wound line carefully inside his can of bait.

He turned to his friend. 'I'm awa,' he said. 'I was tellt to be hame afore it was dark.'

His friend grumbled and protested just as he had known he would. But presently, he, too, wound in his line, and began to put on his stockings and boots. The boy who had seen the cod started off across the rocks, so that his friend would probably hurry to catch up.

He trailed across the rocks slowly, to the base of the cliffs, on top of which several bright, yellow windows now faced the sea. When he turned to look for his friend, it was as if the sea and the sky had got a terrific lot darker all at once. He knew it was because of the contrast with the lighted windows up above.

He fixed his eyes on the windows as he walked along, and through doing that he tripped and let his bait-can fall from his hand to roll down the rocks. His friend began to laugh easily, and called him 'a haddie'. The dry weed exploded with little pops as he crawled about, searching with his flat hand for the line.

When he had found the fishing-line he went on again at once, not bothering about the mussels or the tin which he had had for years. He crumpled the fankled line into a wet ball and held it in his hand with his thumb on the hook. It was no longer cold but had a lukewarm feel by the time they had got in to the foot of the cliffs.

He could feel the sea behind him, and he felt his friend at his side. Then, into his mind where the sea had been putting its cold, dark pictures, came pictures of familiar objects he saw every day without really looking at them. He saw his father's pipes (he had several pipes), his mother's knitting needles, the Libby's calendar that hung up above the mantelpiece, and his own white mug filled with brown tea. They were familiar things but now he saw them as if for the first time.

At the base of the cliffs, where the path began, he stood looking back at the rocks and at the sea. His friend was a couple of paces ahead, because he wanted to get on home and show off his fish. He had his fish laid inside his bait-can, and he looked at them frequently to make sure they were still there.

The boy who had seen the cod raised his finger to point out through the dusk towards the rocks. He called to his friend. He pointed his finger at the big rock where they had gone to fish at the very start. It was covered by the sea. It could just be picked out because the sea was moving over it in a different way than it was doing in the remembered, deeper places, between the rocks.

'Yon's where we were,' he said, pointing carefully. 'Aye, the tide's well in,' his friend said. That was all he said. He wanted to get on home to show his fish.

The other boy saw he did not understand. He stood looking out at the sea without trying to explain what he meant to his friend.

The two boys stood for a moment, looking at the sea. Then the boy who had seen the cod put his arm through his friend's thin, warm arm and they went together up the steep path to the top of the cliffs.

Midsummer Weather

It was damp midsummer weather. There was no breeze. There was a kind of dew on the grass that made it look as if it had been gone over with a thin coat of whitewash, and it lay all day. There was no rain, but in the low sky there were clouds, like great, grey ghosts, wandering to and fro.

For weeks there was no change in the weather. Sometimes a breeze sprang up at night, but each morning, when I wakened, it was eerily still, and the clouds were wandering like ghosts or like soundless zeppelins in the low sky.

It was damp in my working shed. When I glanced up through the window I saw the garden, a dew-wet wilderness thick with nettles and tall, fiery weeds. They stood up straight and still. There was not a breath of wind to stir them even a fraction of an inch.

The pinewoods climbing the edge of the hill had sunk far back till they were like the weird blue mirage of some Eastern town with its cupolas and crosses piled haphazardly against the skyline. The hill between the garden and the woods was white with the dew. Halfway, a lone fir stood as if in a private alcove of grey-dark space.

The weather did not break up. Each day the eerie silence and the dampness of things became more unpleasant. I never went down below, to the strath. I could not think of going fishing either in the dark, dripping wood or on the grey, lonely hill. I longed for autumn, and for one glimpse of a wide, frosted sky filled with stars.

Suddenly, one day no different from all the others, I looked up and saw in the garden a little white lamb. It was like the little white wistful ghost of some poor lamb that had died in the spring. It strayed very silently among the tall, fiery weeds, never bleating.

There was no sign of a mother sheep. It was quite alone, and content.

All day I watched it. It scarcely strayed, as if it was tethered on a cord too fine to see from my window. Not once did it bleat. The little patch of white dwarfed by the weeds, under the low, now oppressive sky, touched my heart. All at once I knew the still weather was drawing to a storm.

That night there was no breeze. In the morning the lamb was still there, in my garden, and during the hours of darkness it had not strayed more than a yard. It was as silent as ever. Around its little white patch, no larger than a pocket handkerchief, all the sadness of the still-born summer seemed to crystallise for me.

I went for the sticks early, in case of the black storm breaking before the afternoon. On the way home I met the shepherd and he said: 'I dropped a lamb in your garden. It has sore feet.'

So the presence of the lamb was explained. It was not a ghost after all.

Afterwards, I went into the garden and stroked its head and fondled its curly, dew-wetted coat. It did not even try to move away on its sore feet. I fetched it water in an old pail.

That day went by. Still the storm did not break. There were strange little thuds. The storm thickened at the backs of the hills invisibly. The dew was almost lukewarm.

The following morning I looked for the lamb as soon as I wakened but I could not see it. At first, I thought it must have strayed farther into the tall weeds, but several hours went by and still there was no sign of its little white patch. I missed it, so I went out presently to see where it had got to. After a little while I found it lying on its side, with its legs stretched out stiffly, among the fiery growth.

I went back to the shed. Now and then I glanced up, and I saw, or felt, the garden to be strangely empty, and strangely still. The tall, fiery weeds were utterly still. But soon, before the first slow, heavy drops of the thunder-rain they began to shiver and sway.

Long after, when the storm was lying far away, on the western horizon, like a great heap of banners and ornamental shells, I went out to the garden to bury the lamb. Carefully, I threw the dark, wet earth on its curly coat, and trod it till it was firm. Then I stood for a while, enjoying the feel of the wind and the fresh smell of the garden.

The Slim, Grey Beauty

Tents, small green and orange triangles, were set among the trees which grew by the side of the burn, near the main road. The trees had rough, black trunks, and the sound of water rushing down among invisible rocks was like red smoke hanging in the air. The tents belonged to camping fishers who had gone away at dawn to fish and had not yet come back, though it was now late afternoon.

Dozens of small, soft, yellow clouds, like wet sheep, had crept across the sky, and presently drops of rain came pattering down through the trees and hit on the tents. The sad sound was swelled by the canvas, and the billycans, blankets, and other pieces of equipment looked as if no one would ever come back for them. In one of the tents lay an accordion, and the keys made a cold mirror for the fading light.

At dusk the fishers came up to the tents, among the dark trees still dripping though the rain had gone off and the sky was clear. They were small, squat town-men, carrying old, slim, fishing rods badly bent towards the tips. The end-flies of the casts were hooked into the handles of the rods, making them bend even more. The fishers did not carry creels but khaki haversacks, hanging heavily, filled with small trout preserved in packings of soft, damp moss.

As soon as they reached the tents, they loosened the guy-ropes, taut, discoloured, like rods of ivory. Then, quickly, they kindled a fire, and in the strange, flickering light began to prepare a meal.

While one man peeled potatoes, a second gutted half the combined catch of little, gold-bellied trout. The third went down to the burn to fill the kettle which, being wet on the outside, began to hiss as the twisting flames licked it with vermilion tongues.

The fishers went silently about their separate tasks, and at the end of an hour they had a rough, excellently-scented meal ready to eat. There was fried trout, boiled potatoes, and sweet, black tea. The three had been fishing since dawn with only pieces in their haversacks so they ate ravenously. Afterwards, they were glad to drink the black tea they had brewed in the kettle and transferred into billys. When they had done, they tapped out round, brown, steaming mounds of tealeaves at their feet.

The fire had burned up well, and now and then there was an explosion like a damp squib among the logs. The twisting flames threw shadows of trees and fishers on the sides of the tents. Stray tree-drops hissed among the hot embers, which soon silenced them.

After a time, the fisher who owned the accordion rose and fetched it from the tent. He sat down carefully, in a place where the trees were not dripping, and buckled it on. He began to play a medley of Scots tunes.

The gold, sunset sound of the accordion stole among the trees, and soon one of the fishers began to add words to the tunes in a low, husky voice. He was a factory worker and there was a considerably quantity of soot in his lungs. His singing was, nevertheless, beautiful, like a spray of wild hawthorn that had been carried away in a newspaper in which a half-dozen briquettes of coal had been previously wrapped. As he sang he stared into the fire with a modest, sad expression.

The third fisher sat apart and did not join in the singing. In silence he looked at the ground where firelight was flickering over pine-needles, fallen twigs, and the little, round, dark balls of sheep-droppings. He smoked a fag that the rain had wetted, and when it went out he lit it again with a glowing twig. The bitter smoke made him cough and screw up his eyes.

The fisher did not feel contented as did his two companions. While he smoked he thought all the time of what had happened that day, of what he had seen while he was away fishing, on his own.

That day, he had been far up the little rushing burn, towards its source on the moor, and in one of the high pools he had seen an enormous trout. At first, he thought it was a water-logged fence-stob, lying at an up-and-down angle on the bed of the stream. He smiled wryly at the ground as he recalled how he had edged his wet-flies carefully around the sunken stob. They had missed it by a mere inch and no more, each time he cast. Then he had seen the stob turn over and show its white belly, taking a fly. When that happened he had given a long, low whistle between clenched teeth.

The great trout refused the fisher's fly, the worm he had then offered it, and even the delicious docken-grub he had found with great difficulty, digging with a rusted shovel in the rubbish-pit of an old, ruined house on the moor. He knew now that he could catch the trout in no other way than by setting a night-line for it. A night-line! He knew it was wrong and he felt a bit ashamed of the idea . . . but . . .

The fisher had done his army service, during the Second World War out East. Once, by accident, he had glimpsed a grey, half-naked foreign girl, crouching. He had not forgotten her, after years. The trout, too, was grey, slim and innocently beautiful. He lusted for it. Now that it had spurned his legitimate advances, its mystery was increased. He had to have it, he felt, by whatever method, and he rose to his feet, meaning to go and set a line to catch it. The two other fishers jerked their heads up, but though their eyes asked where he was off to, they did not speak. The lusting fisher strode silently through the trees, the accordion's sound fading till he could no longer hear it.

Outside, the misted moon was shining palely, and the wide sky was filled with mysterious, silver light. There was silence but for the sheep, like shiny boulders, coughing and bleating in the silver haze lying all around. The fisher felt nervous as he walked, being used to seeing the sky only in narrow strips above the roofs of crowding tenements in the town where he lived. And, thinking of the great trout 'up there', he shivered with excitement. He was used to catching only little trout, averaging about a quarter pound's weight. He followed the burn upwards, hearing its cold melodies ever changing from pool to pool.

It was a long walk up to the pool, and it was almost midnight by the time the fisher had staked his night-line to the bank and returned to the tents. The two occupied tents were snoring heavily. The camp fire was a heap of red ash, faintly wisped with about as much smoke as rises from a cigarette. The fisher crept into his tent, where, breathing a smell of crushed grass and wet canvas, he tried to sleep. On the dark screen of his closed eyes he saw a picture of his night-line, firmly staked and carefully baited. Sometimes he saw it swinging loosely, as the current made it do. Sometimes he saw it drawn out taut by the great fish. At last, after tossing and turning and disordering the neat nest he had made of the blankets, he fell asleep.

During the night the great trout swallowed the worm, and the hook as well, down into its belly at a single gulp. When the pain began, which was almost at once, it swam about in every direction, so far as the staked line would let it go. It broke the surface of the water and thrashed there, in the silver moonlight, for minutes at a time. It swam down to the stony bottom, and roved in half-circles till the thin gut was worn to snapping-point and broke apart. Then it swam away with a slow, peculiar motion, and soon after left the pool.

The fisher wakened with the cold dawn-light coming through the canvas. He turned over, thinking to go back to sleep, then, remembering the line, he sat up suddenly. He cursed himself roundly for having set it. His passion, which had been so fierce a few hours since, was as cold as the grey-ashed campfire outside the tent. He dressed himself slowly, shivering, cursing at buttons as he did them up. Now that his passion was grey-cold ash, he despised it and he felt furious at its consequences. He thought of the long walk he was going to have, away up to the pool and back down again, before breakfast. Day had just broken and it was bitterly cold.

He stepped out from the tent, and as the cold air struck him his arms went goosefleshed. To justify the walk to himself he tried to recall what he had felt about the great trout. He saw it in his mind's eye – merely a big trout without mystery now. 'Ye hoor!' he said to himself, down below his breath, so as not to wake the others who were still asleep and snoring loudly.

A belt of mist, miles long, was lifting from the hills, and the sheep on the moor were moving about like maggots as they cropped. The fisher walked quickly, with a feeling that he had not slept long enough, hating everything. He looked back once, and, seeing smoke rising, he could almost smell the food that would be cooking down below. He knew he would feel better when he was walking the other way, in the right direction, towards his breakfast.

After what seemed a long time he reached the pool, and with only a mild curiosity lifted the line. When he saw the frayed and snapped gut he shrugged his shoulders. Wrenching the stake from the bank, he tossed it and the yards-long line behind him, carelessly. He knew that the following weekend they would be fishing somewhere else, and that they might never be back.

By the time he had made the tents the sun had risen. He was ravenously hungry after his useless walk, and he was pleased to find that some of the breakfast had been kept hot for him, sandwiched between two tin plates laid at the fire's hot fringe of ash. While he ate, the sun sent yellow patches slanting down through the thick trees. His companions, drinking tea and chain-smoking, stood with their backs to the fire, lazily, as if they had been at home in their own tenement kitchens.

At length all three began to dismantle the tents slowly and methodically, and by dinner time they were ready to strike camp. They went down through the trees towards the road, their heavy burdens hoisted on their shoulders, their heads lowered as their eyes followed the thin, twisting path. The campfire, within its circle of blackened stones, grew cold behind them, and sheep came to crop among the trees.

It was about three or four days later that the shepherd saw a limping ewe up on the moor, where the burn was shining. He gave his panting, red-tongued collie the whistle that said to it: 'Go way round.' The dog worked the sheep cleverly towards the shepherd, and at the first opportunity he tripped it with his crook. Saying, 'Wheesht ye, wheesht ye' to the sheep, he unwound the fishing-line that was tangled round one leg, causing it to limp. The sheep struggled while he held it by handfuls of the thick fleece, and as soon as he let go his hold it bolted, bleating.

When later in the same day the shepherd saw the big trout floating belly upwards, among the reeds, he easily guessed what had happened. He kneeled down and turned the fish over to look at it with admiring eyes.

'Ye hoor!' he said, 'ye beauty!' giving his spontaneous judgement on the great fish.

After a time he pushed the fish out into midstream with the handle of his crook, and the current began to trundle it down, jerkily, among the many stones.

Slowly it was borne downwards, big stones dunting it while the whiteness of the belly, in which the hook had fixed, still flashed back at intervals to the man standing up on the bank.

The Potato Planters and the
Old Joiner's Funeral

The potato planters had only just started work again after having their dinner. They were spread out in almost a straight line across their first drills in the middle of the field.

There were seven planters, two men, two women, and three young tinker girls. The old tinker who was carrying the potatoes to them had filled their sack-aprons, and was opening more sacks with his clasp-knife farther down the drills.

The old tinker grimaced when he discovered that all the sacks he opened were filled with big potatoes. That was bad for whoever was carrying to the planters. Before he had got three sacks opened, the seven planters had emptied their aprons and he had to walk back up the drills and fill them all over again. He staggered across the drills, between the planters and the sacks, with the heavy wire basket held at arm's length against his belly.

As soon as they had got their potatoes, the three young tinker girls started to plant them out. They held up their rough heavy sack-aprons as if they were pinafores filled to the brim with pretty flowers. The two men went on planting methodically while the other two women began to move away out in front as if there was a race down to the fence at the bottom of the field.

It was a hot spring day. The seven planters were sweating already. As the tinker said, it was far too hot a day for working: they ought to have been fast asleep under some trees where it was shady and cool. A white heat-haze hung on the hills. The sun was like a huge marigold in the blue sky right above their heads. Away on the far side of the field one of the tractors was droning. The potatoes fell with little thuds into the hot, dry earth where spiders scurried among the grains of the potato manure like cooking salt.

The planters moved slowly down the field, repeating their mechanical movements below the fiery sun that stung their necks. The old tinker filled their sack-aprons with the big potatoes as quickly as he could.

Before the planters had reached the bottom of their first drills they all stopped work for a time and stared down the field to the main road. They stared at the motor hearse going up the road to collect the body of an old joiner who had died that week. They all stared till the black, shiny vehicle went out of sight behind the blue pine trees. The old joiner, they remembered, was to be buried that afternoon at 2.30 in the cemetery on the far side of the village, three miles away. When they had thought about this for several seconds, they all called to have their sack-aprons filled – all seven of them at once.

The tinker ripped open a fresh sack with his clasp-knife. His face was thickly coated with pale dust; it was almost the colour of candle-grease. He leaned his weight on the heavy sack to spill a basket-load of potatoes into the basket at his feet. Before he could get the heavy sack righted again the potatoes had overflowed the basket and spilled on the ground. The old tinker had a sudden melodramatic desire to beat his breast.

Suddenly, while they waited for the old tinker to come with the potatoes, the seven planters noticed that the other old man, who had been carrying potatoes in the morning, was not there. They thought about him not being there and each one, secretly, arrived at the conclusion that he was away at the funeral of the old joiner who was being buried that afternoon at 2.30 in the cemetery at the other side of the village, three miles away. They went on noticing that the old man was not there each time they ran short of potatoes and had to wait for the old tinker to hurry along to them with his heavy basket.

The seven planters reached the bottom of their first drills. They moved into seven new drills and started back up the field. Now they had their backs to the main road and they had an awful feeling that the funeral would sneak by silently without them seeing it. But they had reached the top of the field and turned around again before the funeral went by.

There were more cars than anyone had expected there would be. There were seven cars, not even counting the hearse with the old joiner laid in it, on his way to be buried in the cemetery on the far side of the village, three miles away. The minister's small, streamlined car was in the middle of the line. Because of its shape – like a pullet's egg – it was easy to pick out, and with its bright blue colour it looked very gay among all the other cars that were mostly black. The seven cars kept the same distance apart, and it looked at first as if the hearse was towing them along slowly on one long rope. Then the minister's car started to catch up on the car in front, and the cars in behind it had to hurry to catch up too.

The seven planters stared fixedly at the funeral. Being Protestants they did not cross themselves, or say or do anything whatever. They just stared. The two men did think of raising their caps but it seemed to them that the habit of doing that must have died out. The two women thought of saying something but they were each afraid to speak in case they said the wrong thing. The one in the green apron had a growing feeling that the funeral would have to hurry if it was to be down at the cemetery on the far side of the village by 2.30, as it ought to be.

There was silence for several minutes after the funeral had gone out of sight behind the trees. Then there were seven small thuds because all the seven planters dropped the potatoes they had been holding when they stopped to watch. They started to move on again, in a crooked line, under the hot sun like a huge marigold in the blue sky.

Suddenly the old tinker stopped, and laid his wire basket down on the earth. He bent his knees slightly, and raised his right arm, pointing upwards. The seven planters looked questioningly at him.

'Death!' said the old tinker, waving his left arm about. ''tis terrible what Death will do to a man . . .'

The seven planters stared at the tinker with vacant expressions on their sweaty faces.

'Take that man there,' said the tinker, lowering his arm to point after the funeral. 'I was speaking to that man, there, only on Saturday . . .'

'No,' said the woman in the green apron, firmly, breaking in on the tinker. 'Not that man. Another man. It was a different man, you were speaking to.'

The old tinker let his arm drop down to his side. He turned his face towards the woman in the green apron. Trickles of sweat had drawn tragic lines down his grey cheeks.

'A different man!' he said. 'And is *he* dead as well?'

'They are both dead,' said the woman in green, lowering her sack-apron a little.

'They are both dead. But the man you were speaking to was a different man. I know he was a different man because I saw you speaking to him. I happened to see you speaking to him last Saturday morning, about 10 o'clock, and it was not the same man.'

'A different man!' exclaimed the old tinker, shaking his head sadly. He lifted his basket and staggered towards the planters with it held against his belly.

The half-past bus came out from behind the pine trees with a sudden flash of windows. The planters all stopped planting and looked at the bus going along the main road.

'I thought that,' said the woman in green, 'I knew that all along. It will take that funeral all its time to be down at the cemetery by half-past two.'

One of the two men planters took his watch out slowly, looked at it intently, then put it away. The seven planters moved down the field in the intense heat. They reached down to the bottom of the drills and turned up again.

A few minutes later there was a further interruption as a tractor came racing into the potato field through the far gate. The trailer was loaded high with more potato-sacks and on the top of the load stood the gay young tinker, the old tinker's son. He stood with his legs wide apart, lashing the tractor with a long, imaginary whip. Plainly, he was imagining himself to be a cossack or something.

'Tallyho! Crack! Crack! Yipee!' he kept on shouting at the top of his voice.

The old tinker scowled when he discovered that the new sacks, too, were filled with big potatoes. He seemed to see two old men stretched out under shady trees, and though one of them, he knew, was different he could not think why that was the case.

The hot sun, like a huge marigold, beat down on the field.

The other old man, who was away at the funeral, did not get back to the potato field till almost four o'clock. The old tinker asked him where he had been.

The Old Man and the Trout

He was a tenant of a red-roofed cottage where we spent a summer holiday once. I suppose I must have been about eleven or twelve years old at the time. It was late on in the summer evenings the old man used to spin me his sleepy yarns. While he yarned we sat together on his wooden garden-bench, in view of his green and yellow honeysuckle bushes full of late-shift bees. Behind us was a big field of ripening corn, with a lot of poppies like blood-spatters in it, bright crimson in the rusty gold. The old man sat well forward, his vein-knotted arms laid flat along his trousers which were pulled up tight, showing his carefully polished boots.

I can't remember much of what the old man said. Mostly he talked about his mole-trapping days, or about his own boyhood, when he'd lived down South. He still had a trace of the Southern way of talking and it was perhaps that that gave his voice such a tickly, sleepy sound. But somehow the mole-trapping was not true to the old man's character as I saw it. A lot of things I said or did would bring a momentary clot of sadness into his hazel eyes.

Once I talked the old man into taking me out fishing. I made him give a solemn promise to catch me a trout. I couldn't catch a trout myself, hard as I tried, every day. Still, the fish there were lovely to look at – fat and sleek, though a bit on the fly side, I thought.

When the old man had said he would take me fishing, we went round to the back of the cottage to gather worms from the hen-coop. The coop was round in the long, narrow garden the old man looked after, with the help of his sister, who was tying string round the currant bushes just then, as we began to dig the worms. The old man suffered from rheumatism, so he held the worm-tin while I dug at the dunged soil with a fork.

It must have been a very hot day, for I remember the old man had first unbuttoned his waistcoat, then taken it off and hung it on a bush. His woolly vest showed white through the slits in his thick, grey shirt. Once I broke a worm in half as I was pulling it from its escape-hole, and he stepped forward and ground the bits to nothing with his polished boot. 'They have feelings the same as we do,' he said, looking at me gently. As he spoke, the apple in his throat wobbled up and down, and I was suddenly saddened to see the brown crinkles in his neck, where his shirt-collar was missing. Then his sister called over to him from among the currant-bushes, and while he was gone to help her knot the string, I gathered up the worms and we were ready to start.

I took my rod from the shed where I always left it, never taking the pieces down, or untying the hook. It was an old shed. In the dusty corners of it stood cobwebbed washing-mangles, and the kind of big, brass basins in which blackcurrant jam is made in season. There was a steady drip of sunlight through the tiles down to the floor of brown earth. I liked just to stand in there, sniffing the dusty-damp smell which reminded me of something – something I could almost, but never quite remember.

The blue tar on the road had melted in the heat, and I left the marks of my rubber-heeled shoes on it as I walked along. At first, the old man carried the fishing rod while I was left to carry the tin of worms. It was an old treacle tin with a tight-fitting lid in which I had made a few holes with a hammer and nail. 'They have to breathe the same as we do,' I thought of the old man saying. I carried the tin inside my shirt to keep the worms cool and wet. I was scared they might close up like accordions and become no good for the trout.

It was almost no distance from the cottage down to the stream. On the way, though, we had to go by the Big House. Just as we drew level with the lawn, with its neat rhododendron bushes, the old man put the fishing rod into my free hand, and looked away into the fields on the other side of the road, as if he had caught sight of something. I could not see anything there myself. He took back the rod as soon as we were by the Big House and in sight of the stream.

Now that I could see the water running out from the bridge, I thought it might be better after all if it was me who fished. But I waited behind the old man while he slowly climbed the fence. Then we began to make our way down the bank of the stream which was grown all over with a strange kind of weed, like garden rhubarb that had jumped a wall and gone wild. This weed, said the old man, would hide us from the trout.

Instead of starting to fish right away, as I knew we ought to, we walked on down to the deep corner pool. There, the old man stopped, and soon we sat down among the false rhubarb. Flies buzzed round us noisily. A motor-bicycle whizzed up the road, leaving its sound spread out behind it like a long, black snake.

The pool was dappled on the far side with the shadows of trees. The clear water, as it swirled among their roots, was soiled by a drain that poured out rusty stuff, the colour of spate. It certainly was a fine place to fish the worm. I knew that several big trout lived under the trees, for I had often seen them feeding there, from the other bank. They always ignored the worms I threw down to them, except when I threw just the worms without the hook.

At length, the old man screwed himself up to spear on a worm. He told me to sit still where I was, and not to stand up, or shout, or I would scare the fish. Then he began to crawl towards the pool carrying the rod in one hand, and, with the other, clearing away the stems of the weed. The big green leaves kept closing back like the sea. I had to stand up just a little to see him cast. He threw the worm out in a way I thought terribly clumsy. It fell just by luck, though, in the mouth of the drain and began to float down slowly into the shadow of the trees.

To my surprise, the old man laid down the rod with its tip balanced on the edge of the rhubarb leaf. He crawled back towards me, and I could feel him creak. Seeing that I had half-stood up, he waved his hand at me, and I dropped down so as not to spoil his crazy fishing. At the same time I kept my eye on the tip of the rod. Almost at once, it was jerked down from the leaf. A trout had taken the worm. I shouted, and the old man stood up and made a grab for the butt.

Except once in a fishmonger's shop, I had never been so near to a big trout. While the old man wound hurriedly at the handle of the reel, the trout followed upstream in a slow, aloof sort of way. At first, I thought he was going to snag the gut on the barbed-wire cattle-fence which ran aross the shallow water at the top of the pool. But he suddenly turned and swam back down towards the roots of the trees. He could not quite reach them because of the dragging line. He leaped out from the water with a big splash then surprised us both by swimming almost to our feet. I could see the red spots on his sides, and his baleful eyes. Then he swam away again, taking the slack of the line.

While the trout splashed in the water, in the shadow of the trees, the old man looked around for a place to land him but there was simply nowhere. The banks were steep, and we had no landing-net. It was a rotten situation.

At length the fish began to turn sideways on the top of the water, and the old man reeled him across the pool till he lay right below us. He lay almost on his back, with his mouth opening slowly and regularly as a clock ticks at night. All at once I felt sorry for him and I wished we had him on the bank.

The old man handed me the rod, and began to push up his jacket sleeve to above his elbow. Then he kneeled down over the trout, and closed his fingers on it, below the gills. He was raising it from the water when suddenly it slipped, and he was left holding only the gut, broken off a good way above the hook. I dropped the rod and looked after the fish as it swam away, with my hook in it.

The old man stood quite still for several minutes, looking after the trout. Then I picked up the rod and the worm-tin, and we walked up the road to the house, saying not a word to each other. I was worried about losing the hook but, as it happened, I had another one hidden away among the hankies in my drawer. I stopped worrying. I went in for my tea, and while I was eating I saw the old man's stooped figure across the window, and I heard his chair scrape back as – it must have been – he took off his boots.

When I had finished my tea, I went out and sat on the bench sort of waiting for the old man. He didn't come, so in the end I went along and knocked on his door. It was his sister who answered my knock. She was wiping her red hands on a white dish-cloth, while behind her I could see the wallpaper with its pattern of faded roses, and a wooden coat-stand with a pair of the old man's galoshes down below. She took me through to the kitchen where the old man was sitting in a chair drawn in by the fire.

When he saw me come in he sat up. A grey shawl was thrown about his shoulders. He had taken to his stocking-soles to ease his feet, and his boots were laid by in the hearth, the firelight dancing on the polished leather. His sister told me he got the rheumatism from being down at the stream fishing, but the old man said it was a sure sign of rain. That cheered me up.

I did not wait long in the old man's private kitchen. He was going to bathe his feet in a papier-mâché basin which his sister carried through from the scullery, and put down for him on the woolly rug. I waited only till she had filled the basin. I heard him groan as he bent forward to drag off his socks; and afterwards, when I was in the garden, I heard the water gurgling away mysteriously down the hidden drain.

Sure enough, there was rain as the old man's rheumatism prophesied. The big drops splashed on the honeysuckle bushes, outside the window, all night. I woke up early. After breakfast, though, it was still raining and I wasn't allowed to go out. Then in the afternoon it faired up, and I was let to take my rod from the shed, with its new, puddled floor. The smell in there was a whole lot different that day – sad and exciting somehow. I didn't have to waste time digging for worms. They had come up to the top of the ground, and one or two of the pink ones wriggled across the road and were squashed thinly on the blue tar. All I had to do was to lift them up.

The sunlit water looked like lentil soup. Twigs and other things were bobbing round in black-ripples, and I let my worm drop in beside them and I caught a good trout. I ran back across the fields and gave it in to the old man. His sister was pleased. She put the fish on a white platter, with little bits of green grass still sticking to its red-spotted sides. I went in to stare at it several times before it was gutted and fried.

The next day the water was almost clear again and I couldn't get any bites. I went down, after a while, to the corner pool, to see if I could spot the big trout. I saw one big fish, but I didn't think it was him, so I went on down to the next pool, and the next one again. This pool was like a big deep hole, with a lot of rotten branches half-buried in the mud down at the bottom of it. It was a pool where you could easily lose all your hooks.

I was just going to walk right by the pool, as I usually did, when my eye caught on something that was glinting down on the mud. I clambered down the bank and picked up a dead branch which snapped. I threw it away. When I had found a branch strong enough, I thrust it down through the water, and poked at the big fish to get him where I could lift him out. Little pieces of mud flaked off the bottom and whirled round him like smoke. He sank up and down like a balloon each time I thrust. When at last I was able to get hold of him, I dropped him on the bank and he was quite stiff. A blue-bottle came and crawled on his eye but I shooed it away.

After I had looked at him for a long time, I took out my penknife and got back my hook. It was a little rusted, of course, but there was enough of the bloodied gut left to tie back on my line. I wondered what I ought to do with the trout and, eventually, I pushed him into a hole in the bank and pulled the long grass down on top.

When I had done fishing and got back to the house, the old man was sitting out on the garden bench waiting for me. His rheumatism was a bit better, and he yarned for a while about moles, and said it was an awful pity we'd lost the big trout. It was on the tip of my tongue to tell him what had happened, but I never did for I guessed that if I had it would have broken his heart.

The Fight in the Ditch

It was autumn. They were carting turnips in from the fields. Row upon row of turnips lay like dim, smoky lanterns on the black earth.

Big Dod, one of the farm-workers, was shawing turnips in the field. A tall, slim, angular man with a dark moustache and white teeth, he looked, as he gripped his turnip-knife, like some kind of wild Corsican brigand. His old khaki greatcoat, now dyed to a dark colour, reached almost to his boots.

The field was hidden from the farm steading by a bulge in the brown woods. The hills to either side were misted. The autumn silence was broken only by the cawing of rooks and by the rustling of the wet turnip shaws and the solemn dumping of the turnips, like the slow, regular ticking of a grandfather clock, as they fell to the ground.

Big Dod, though he was left alone there, worked without halt, moving quickly up one drill and down another, so that half the field, now, was softly alight with stripped turnips. He did not straighten up to ease his bent back, knowing that to do so would surely have made the dull ache worse.

Then, halfway up one drill, Big Dod abruptly stood up straight, and listened. There was a new sound beside him in the turnip field, and he could not tell what it was or where it came from.

He listened carefully. His head turned this way and that, slowly, like an aircraft predictor, as he tried to catch the sound. A full minute went by before he was able to tell what the new sound was.

At the top of the field lay a ditch. About a week since the ditch had been in spate with the autumn rains, but now the water, flowing in the wood's shadow, was thin and clear again. The transparent autumn water looked as if it might have dripped from the moon.

There was a great trout in the ditch. Having swum up the ditch to spawn when the water was swollen it had somehow got stranded there. It splashed in the long, shining, shallow ripple above the plank-bridge, but it would never force its way across the ripple in a million years.

Big Dod listened, and suddenly he recognised the sound for what it was. He grinned. Then, thrusting his turnip-knife in below his armpit, he strode up the drills, carrying the known sound in his head like a pebble with a large label tied to it.

On the edge of the ditch Big Dod stopped, and he looked down on the great trout. The trout saw the tall, dark man tower above it, and in a flash it moved.

The trout splashed free of the ripple, and swam slowly up the narrow, deep stretch of water beyond. Twelve yards up the ditch it turned again, and, like a caged panther taking exercise, paced back down with slowly rippling fins.

Twelve yards was all the length of the great trout's cage, for there was an old wooden sluice, coated with dead leaves, at the far end, and the ripple sealed the other. The great trout was trapped. It paddled restlessly to and fro up and down its cage.

Big Dod showed his white teeth in a broad grin. With a sudden movement he took his turnip-knife from below his armpit and flung it to the ground, where the sharp blade buried itself to the hilt.

A moment later he began to unbutton his greatcoat. He wrenched off the coat, and he threw it, too, to the ground. He had challenged the great trout to a fight in the ditch.

As Big Dod sprang, the water rose up in a jagged white splash against the dark wood. It was so cold it seemed to scald him, and he cursed the trout. As soon as the water had settled he saw the trout down below him, poised on the edge of the ripple.

Big Dod went for his adversary. As he moved his mouth fell open, as if he meant to gobble the fish alive when he had got his hands on it. Instinctively, he crouched, and the seat of his pants drew a long, fine line down the glassy surface of the water that reached almost to his thighs. He held his hands out before him as a wicket-keeper does when he is waiting for a catch.

Big Dod moved down towards the ripple. He kept his eyes fixed on the skulking trout. The trout waited, watching, only flickering its fins to balance itself on the press of the stream.

Then Big Dod grabbed. But such was the speed of the trout that he never saw it. It flashed by his legs. Two brief balls of bitter-cold water slid though his fingers and left them stinging with white pain. When he next saw the trout it was eyeing him warily from the sluice-end of the cage.

Big Dod leaped to the bank. He cursed the trout for its cowardly tactics, then he sat down, considering. His eye fell on the turnip-knife, and he reached for it.

Big Dod looked at the knife, then, narrowing his eyes, he drew the blade gently across the ball of his thumb. For an instant the precise cut kept its perfection, then the blood gushed out from it and Big Dod tenderly sucked the thumb. At the same time he whistled the proven blade through the air.

But a moment later he let the knife drop from his hand. His face clouded. He dimly sensed the weapon was too subtle to bridge the gulf between water and air, and to kill across it. He stared at the trout with a puzzled expression, trying to measure that gulf.

All at once, as he stared at the trout and saw its pale, cold eye still so fearless, like the dial of a machine, his strength began to flood down his arms, and into his fists. Then, beyond his fists, he felt it bud into great impalpable half-ton weights, with which to smash.

Big Dod rose to his feet. He began to look around for something heavy with which to smash the trout. It was several minutes before he saw the boulders embedded all along the edge of the field.

The boulders had been carried up there from all over the field to be out of the way of the plough. There was a great number of them. When Big Dod began to see them his eyes lit up with satisfaction. He started to gather some into a pile on the edge of the ditch.

Since he was accustomed to carrying two-hundredweight corn-sacks up the steep stairs to the granary, the weight of the boulders meant little to Big Dod.

When he had rocked each boulder free of the earth, he embraced it, raised it to the level of his chest, and carried it over to the ditch. There he set it down.

When he had over a dozen boulders in a heap on the bank Big Dod stopped. He looked down at the trout that was paddling to and fro, more than ever like a caged panther, with slow fins. Big Dod impulsively spat at the great sleek fish.

Then he began to measure the gulf in terms of muscle-power and the weight of his boulders. After a time he raised the first boulder to the level of his chest and threw. He did not merely drop the boulder: he threw it. As soon as he had thrown the first boulder he lost sight of the trout.

Big Dod hurled the boulders one after another, in quick succession, blindly. Around each boulder rose four or five perfect water-petals, each as large as many gallons of water that were lost to the ditch. The white petals fell, some to this side, some to that, and faded into the ground. The splashing and the bashing of boulder on boulder in the bed of the ditch made a great din.

At last, Big Dod had hurled all the boulders and he waited, panting a little, for the disturbed water to clear. The mud flowed away downstream, and the ditch grew transparent again. Big Dod grinned when he saw his weapons had smashed across that gulf.

By then the great trout had turned over on its belly. With feeble thrusts of its sidefins it swam backwards in half-circles that each traced the shape of a waning moon in the ditch. Often it collided clumsily with one or other of the banks.

All at once Big Dod was on the top of the maimed trout, and he tossed it ashore. There, he leaped on it, stunned it, and proceeded to smash it properly so that its delicate works broke loose and were strewn all around. Then he looked at what was left of the trout and he threw it below the hedge where the keeper would not see it if he came by the field.

Big Dod picked up his greatcoat and he began slowly to button it on. But, finding that his fingers were too chilled to cope with the buttons, he left them unfastened. Then he picked up his turnip-knife and made his way back down the field and began to shaw turnips again.

All the rest of the day, till dusk, he kept thinking it must be pay-day, though it was really only the middle of the week. That was how he interpreted the satisfaction he felt at having disposed of the great trout.

Once again there was no sound in the field save the cawing of the rooks, and the rustling of the wet turnip-shaws and the solemn dumping of the turnips as they fell to the earth behind Big Dod.

Over the Sharp Stones

The summer evening was almost at an end. The sun was setting now. The old man was carrying a load of firewood up the steep, stony road that was like the bed of a dried-up burn. It was as if he was trudging slowly up into the sunset that hung, flaring brightly, at the top of the brae.

Rivulets of light trickled down the road, turning the sharp stones, some of which were as big as small boulders, to a lurid crimson colour. Here and there, to either side of the road, stood full-grown firs, outlined against the setting sun. To one side, hiding the deep valley down below, lay a large wood, now a deep-green colour, almost black, but somehow deeper than black. The top of the road seemed to be melting into the centre of the sun.

Halfway up the steep hill the old man grew breathless and his squat, dark shape came to a stop. He eased the bundle of logs off his hip-bone, where he had it balanced, and set it down on the road. Then, panting, he took a crumpled white silk handkerchief from his pocket and began to mop his brow.

As if it was badly cut, the old man's jacket hung down awkwardly to the one side. When he went to replace the handkerchief, it swung out and then in again on the hinge of the bottom button. In the inside pocket, just large enough to hold it, lay a heavy gin-trap, like a piece of abstract sculpture cast in metal, with the title 'Agony'.

Having mopped his brow, the old man stuffed the handkerchief away. He put his hand to the breast of the jacket, fingering the hard bulge of the trap through the thick cloth to make sure it was safe. As he did so, he frowned, and muttered to himself angrily. Then, letting his short, stumpy arms drop to his sides, he stared around idly, waiting to get his breath back for the rest of the climb up to his house.

The air was fresh and cool. The light was dimming. Shadows gathered in the roadside ditch. Rabbits ran in circles and leaped playfully in front of the wood where there was an area of flat ground, covered with clumps of rushes and coarse grass. The old man's eye came to rest on the rabbits. Several seconds later, showing their white tails like pinches of cotton wool, they ran away. The lowest fence-wires twanged as the rabbits darted through the fence on the way to their burrows on the edge of the wood.

All was still for a moment. Then there was a sudden crunching of footsteps. A few loose stones slithered down the steep road and stopped in ruts. The underkeeper came striding out of the sunset and was suddenly there.

Nodding, the keeper stopped by the old man. He had his gun on his shoulder and his canvas game-bag, with the red-brown net on the outside of it dangling empty, was slung across his back. After a moment he lowered the gun, and, leaning on the crimson-streaked blue barrel as if on a walking-stick, he said: 'Aye, aye.'

'Aye, aye,' answered the old man, returning the customary greeting. As soon as he had spoken he lowered his eyes and fixed them firmly on the stones at his feet. There was wet grit between the stones. Without shifting the soles of his boots from the stones the old man carefully put himself farther away.

'It's a fine night . . .' began the keeper. He stared into the sky, above the wood, twisting his hand in his moustache. The moustache, brown in colour but scorched by match-flames and encrusted with little particles of dried soup, drooped over his lips. His eyes were cruel but simply for the same reason that a ploughman's hands are hard-skinned: on account of his trade.

The old man made no reply to the keeper's remark. He remained standing silently, like a dead tree-stump or a dark, moss-covered boulder, heavy on the grey road. The sunset was fading. As the light dimmed, the road paled, and torrents of cold, white silence came swirling down it, surrounding the two men.

The keeper pulled at his moustache. He cleared his throat several times, wanting to speak but unable to speak because of the way the old man stood with his eyes unavailable, firmly fixed on the sharp stones.

Then one of the fence-wires twanged. A rabbit that had been clapped down among the rushes had made a sudden dash for its hole, leaping through the fence.

At once, the old man jerked his head up and the keeper seized on his eyes. 'I was wondering,' he said in a weak voice, 'if you saw a trap of mine. I lost a trap – over there.' Taking his hand out of his moustache, he waved across at the flat ground in front of the wood.

The wood, now, was soft, sooty-black in colour, the tallest of the evergreens thrusting up from the middle of it like slender masts and ship-cranes, silhouetted against the pale, evening sky. The sun had dropped out of sight behind the top of the brae.

The old man looked across at the flat ground, pitted with shadows. He did not answer at once. He seemed to think deeply, and, perhaps to prove it, he raised the brim of his cap and scratched his head. After a long time he drew his lips together and sucked his breath in with a long, slow negative sound that made the keeper give a sigh. The old man sighed also. 'I saw no trap,' he said. 'Maybe a dog went off with it,' he added. 'Maybe a sheep did.' He shrugged his thick, square shoulders and stared at his boots.

The keeper put his hand back to his moustache, pulling at it again, drawing it even more out of shape. 'I thought you might have chanced on that trap,' he said, but the old man only shrugged and stepped back slightly, his boots scrunching on the wet grit and his weighted jacket swinging out and then in. Then the keeper too took a small step backwards, and he shouldered his gun. The two men drew apart.

'Good-night, then,' said the keeper.

'Good-night to you,' said the old man. Bending forwards he grasped his load of firewood, raised it up, and set it on his hip, manoeuvring it an inch or so forwards and backwards till it rested like a see-saw on the protruding bone. Stepping sideways by the old man, the keeper started down the brae.

The old man climbed upwards slowly. The keeper watched his dark shape ascend into the pale sky and vanish. But at the top of the road two further hills and a long pinewood, as well as the low-set cottage, came into sight. The topmost branches of the wood lay like hundreds of small, ecclesiastical crosses against the light in the west.

The old man came to the front door of the cottage. He dropped his load of wood. When he had got his breath back he walked slowly to the end of the house where a wooden shed, with a tin roof, had been built on.

He pushed on the door of the shed. It opened with a creak. Behind the door was pitch-darkness, smelling of wet sacks, raw earth, and stagnant Time. There was one small window up in the roof but it was thick with dust. The old man's three hens, startled by the sound of the door opening, gave low croons of alarm.

Feeling his way forward with slow and heavy feet, the old man crossed to the corner of the shed that was nearest the open door. He took the gin-trap from his pocket and let it fall through the darkness. There was a loud clank! Now there were eleven instead of ten stolen gin-traps in a heap on the raw earth. The old man turned and felt his way out of the shed.

'Cruel things,' he muttered to himself self-righteously. 'Cruel things them gin-traps are.' He wiped his hands down the sides of his jacket as if to clean them of the trap's cruelty, and went into the house through the low door.

In a few moments he had the Aladdin oil-lamp lighted. The small kitchen with its low, smoke-blackened ceiling and smoke-blued wooden mantelshelf, was filled with soft light the colour of July corn. A bunch of red and gold onions hung from the ceiling, scenting the air with bitterness. Several pots coated with soft soot like a kind of fur stood by the open fire, on the bricks. One of them, the stew-pot, was filled with cold water to steep.

Having poked the fire up, the old man filled the kettle, and set it on the twisted flames. He ate a slice of bread spread with cheese and onion, and drank a cup of sweet, black tea. When he had done, he wiped his mouth with the back of his hand, and crossed over to the door. He listened, his head to one side, then sat down again, lighting his pipe with a paper spill from the ash in the hearth.

There was silence in the room save for the old man's heavy breathing and the slow ticking of the tin alarm-clock. Blue smoke floated upwards and hung in curls around the red onions. When the clock had measured sufficient time, the old man stood up.

Taking his walking-stick from behind the door, he went out of the house.

The thin, round moon had risen clear of the opposite hills. The old man, who was sure the keeper would have set his new trap and gone home, did not find it difficult to see his way. He went directly to where the new trap was set in front of the dark wood.

There was a deep and silver silence. The shadow thrown by the wood fell several yards short of the newly set trap. The two metal teeth, protruding from the scraped earth, gleamed dully. Catching sight of the teeth, the old man moved warily, and shook his free fist, clenching the other so tightly on the stick that the knuckles shone.

Taking his stick in two hands, he pressed down with the point of it, springing the trap. The teeth came together with a sharp and vicious sound, scaring a pigeon from inside the wood into the light air. The bird flew away.

For several minutes the old man stood by the sprung trap, staring down at it with deep dislike. Then, with a last, fierce and scornful glance at it, he turned and crossed quickly into the shadow of the wood. He began to set his rabbit-snares one after another in the good runs in the long grass over by the fence. When he had set the customary number of snares he turned back to the house. Smoke curled from the squat chimney. The whitewashed triangle of the gable-end glimmered in the light of the moon.

In the middle of the moonlit night, the old man wakened once and sat up in bed. His eyes falling on the stew-pot, he listened, hearing the shrill, white squeals of a rabbit caught in a snare. For several seconds, his eye on the black stew-pot, he listened. Then, smiling tenderly, he lay down and at once fell fast asleep.

Advice from the Author

One winter morning, when the ground was white, and my kitchen was filled with the dark brown smell of infusing coffee, I received a typewritten letter from a well-known author asking me if I would care to do the illustrations to his new fishing book. I was only too pleased to send a pre-paid telegram saying that I would visit him in Edinburgh the following day as his letter suggested. I borrowed my train fare from the shepherd, knowing it would be returned to me, and when I went to bed that night I set my alarm-clock to waken me at six in the morning.

At that hour it was pitch-dark. There was only a narrow strip of dawn light in the dark sky, a sickly, white, fascinating strip behind the branches of the pines. I ate my breakfast without appetite, and with that sense of melodrama which arises from all journeys, even short journeys, that start before dawn.

When I arrived in Edinburgh, via the Forth Bridge, it was after midday. I had changed into three separate trains, with a long, cold wait between each. Having only seven shillings in the world I thought I would take a taxi to the well-known author's house. The Poor can easily afford to be extravagant, like the Very Rich.

When I got down from the taxi I had no difficulty in finding the address I had in my pocket. The door-front was imposing. I jerked the large brass bell-handle. After several minutes my ring was answered by an elegant lady who, I naturally supposed, was the well-known author's wife. I gave my name and waited to be invited in.

My name only gave rise to a puzzled expression. I repeated it again, more loudly, because trams and lorries were making a noise in the street at my back. The lady beckoned me into the hall. I repeated my name a third time and she began to wring her pale, elegant hands. I took out the piece of paper on which I had copied the address, and in which I had carefully wrapped all the money that was left after paying for the taxi. As I handed her the paper the coins fell to the floor and rolled away under tables and chairs. There were any number of halfpennies. I felt silly as I got down on my hands and knees and recovered a fair weight of coins which I stuffed back in my pocket. When the lady had deciphered the address her face brightened. She explained to me, in halting English, that there were two such addresses in that district and I had unluckily come to the wrong one. The one I wanted was a little way up the street on the opposite side.

I had carefully asked the taxi-driver not to stop in front of the well-known author's house. I thought he would probably go around in tram-cars, being comfortably off, and might not understand my arriving in a taxi when I was too poor, he had been told, to pay my own train-fare. To my horror, I found that his house was exactly opposite where the taxi had stopped to avoid stopping opposite his house. I stood between two stone shrubs and rang the bell.

The door was answered almost at once by a tall, thin, bony, young man, with leather patches on the elbows of his jacket. I opened my mouth and pronounced my mystic name. The young man vanished and when he came back, five minutes later, I was invited to enter the hall. The young man halted, leaned forward and whispered in my ear.

'He is ill,' he whispered, 'but you may come upstairs and talk to him. Follow me.'

I followed the young man closely across the hall, but going up the stairs I fell behind. They were difficult stairs. To mount them one stair at a time was almost ridiculous, but two stairs were just an inch or two higher than I could possibly stretch. The young man, I noticed, had the stairs mastered. He swung up ahead of me, thrusting his thin, bony elbow through the banister, using it as a lever to hoist himself up several stairs at a time, with great swings and leaps. When I tried the same method, my elbow stuck in the banister. The young man stood watching me at the head of the stairs, smiling faintly.

The famous author lay in bed, convalescing from his illness. There was a gas fire with orange flames and the room was warm without being stuffy, while the window was filled with the dim, grey cold light of the winter afternoon. The famous author shook my unknown hand and I sat down on a chair by the side of his bed. Almost at once he leaned over to a little table and took a finger-sip of snuff from a little silver box. I waited several seconds for his enormous sneeze but no sneeze came. I asked if he would mind my smoking, and while I lit a Woodbine he told me about the illness that had only recently been driven from his chest. I began to feel the illness, at bay, in the room. I imagined it hiding in below the bed ready to jump out and sink its teeth into my trousers, or to creep up on me from behind. I tucked my legs uneasily in below the chair.

'I think,' said the well-known author, 'you will be the very person to illustrate my book.'

I smiled modestly.

'You *can* draw fishing scenes?' he asked.

I was taken aback. I thought this fact had already been established before he wrote to me. Having prepared a speech on the subject of fishing, from my personal viewpoint, I decided to try to fit it in here. It was a long, involved speech. I had composed it in the train. It had definitely to do with fishing, but from my own point of view, and it began obscurely.

'Life,' I said, making it plain that the word had a capital, 'is a raw tragedy. To create from that tragedy, to distill from that tragedy, to make of that tragedy . . .'

I could not remember what I had been going to say. It had all been quite clear in the train. Now, I could only think of the isolated words such as 'sadness', 'Schopenhauer', 'rainy-pools', 'art' and 'spate'. I waved my hand.

'I see what you mean,' said the well-known author, and he lifted the bulky manuscript of his book from the table by the bed.

'I have written,' he said, 'a most unusual fishing book, and I am sure *you* will be the very person to illustrate it.'

While he flicked over the pages of the book, he asked again: 'You *can* draw men fishing?'

'Yes,' I said simply, abandoning my speech.

The author's eye was suddenly caught by one of his own paragraphs. He began to roar with laughter, slapping his sides and rolling about the bed.

'Listen to this,' he said, when he had slightly recovered. He began to read aloud from the book. He had read only a few sentences when he again became helpless with laughter. I smiled. I thought of my own sad drawings, and I wondered if I really was the person to illustrate his book. When he had stopped laughing he read me several pieces from the manuscript, quite lengthy pieces, and then he looked at me and said: 'Short of disaster, your drawings will be accepted by my publisher.'

I remembered that sentence later when my drawings were turned down.

At the close of the interview the famous author gave me careful instructions as to how to catch a tram to the railway station. I caught a tram this time, in case I was being watched, and I was at the station just in time to catch the last train of the day to my part of the country. There was only one other person in my compartment, a middle-aged woman who stared at me more frequently as the minutes went by.

I do not particularly like beards, but at this time, in mid-winter, I had a small beard, as the negative result of not shaving for several weeks. My hair, also, was rather in need of a trim. I was, therefore, surprised when my travelling companion leaned forward and said: 'You are an artist, aren't you now? You may wonder how I know. The fact is, I can see *through* you. I am psychic.' I smiled politely.

'Let me see your hand,' said the lady, leaning forward in her seat.

I held out my hand, palm upwards, while she drew the tip of her finger slowly along the various lines. I began to laugh.

'Don't you believe in hand-reading?' she said.

'Absolutely,' I said, 'it's just that you're tickling me.'

She traced her finger all the way down my life-line and I snatched away my hand. I am terribly tickly. I couldn't stand it.

'Just as I thought,' she said, 'you are very quick-tempered. You have a stubborn will.'

'You will be a famous artist,' she added – I smiled – 'when you are dead!'

Dark fields, not yet ploughed, whirled by the window. There was one small light in the carriage, a small bulb about the size of a torch-bulb, up in the roof. The light was noticeably poor.

'Not all the darkness in the world,' the lady said, 'can dim the light of one small candle.'

'Very good,' I said, looking at her with genuine admiration. It was only later I discovered the aphorism was one of Confucius's. I thought it was one of her own.

In the next few days, I read the well-known author's manuscript, and made several drawings. I sent the drawings off by post, and waited to see if the famous author would think them suitable, before making more, as I was keen to do.

His reply came back by return of post. He liked the drawings, but there were just one or two small points that had him worried. One of these was that I had drawn him as a small boy, looking about nine years old, whereas the manuscript clearly stated that he was only seven and a half. A second point was that I had sketched him looking down into a trout-pool, but would the reader, he asked me, be quite sure to know it *was* a trout-pool? Where, in fact, were the trout? I answered this point by quoting his own words, which stated there was a Mystery down in the trout-pool. I explained that I had drawn the Mystery, but if he wanted me to draw the trout I could do that instead. I could even draw two pools, one with a Mystery in it, and the other with trout. But, I could not draw him, aged seven and a half, looking down at both the trout *and* the Mystery at the same time. That was beyond my limited powers.

The well-known author replied that these were only small points. They could be settled later. Meanwhile, he had forwarded my drawings to his publisher with a strong recommendation that I be allowed to go ahead. I sighed with relief. And I heard no more about the drawings until, two weeks later, they were returned to me with a note saying they were hopelessly unsuitable. The air was brown with coffee and the white ground rang below the postman's feet as he walked away from the door. I was back where I had started, more or less, except that I still had several halfpennies to jingle in my pocket, owing to the famous fishing author's most helpful advice about the tram.

Encounter

The fisherman was squatting on his heels in front of the campfire, holding his billycan to the flames on the end of a branch. He stared at the can intently, whistling to himself softly and tunelessly through parted lips. The water in the can was almost on the boil.

Above the fire was an almost vertical bank of dark, moist earth, to which the fisherman's thickset back was turned. At the top of the bank were pine trees, the sky showing in grey, faintly glistening rectangles between their dark trunks. On the still, damp evening at the end of the summer the trees seemed lifeless; it was as if the slim trunks were filled with thick, stagnant ditchwater instead of living sap.

The steep bank cast its shadow across the fisherman as he squatted almost motionlessly on his heels by the fire. There was a smell of damp earth and decaying undergrowth, the rural equivalent of the smell of a city slum. The woodsmoke rose in thick white clouds, lingering and melting among the trees above.

Now and then, as the smoke rolled back on the fisherman, he wiped his smarting eyes with his dark-blue sleeve. He would disappear momentarily into a drift of pale smoke, in his dark-blue clothes. When the smoke had cleared again he was still in the same position, half-buried in the loose, wet shadow at the bottom of the bank, his eyes on the can.

For a long time the water hesitated on the verge of boiling. Then at last, it broke into sudden, violent movement, splashing over the sides of the can and sizzling on the red, incandescent mass of embers into which the fire had dwindled. The fisherman grinned.

Reaching into his jacket pocket with his left hand, he drew out a pink football coupon envelope filled with tea and sugar, speckled grains, already mixed together. He shook the envelope over the can, and set it down by the edge of the embers, slipping the branch from the handle and tossing it on the ground.

The tea infused and darkened till, in colour, it resembled a little mountain pool, red-brown with yellow froth afloat on top. When the tea had stood long enough, the fisherman, still squatting on his heels, began to drink. He drank the hot tea with long, slow, noisy sips, squinting vacantly by the brim of the can. The rosy glow of the ashes fell on his brow, from which the hair had receded and where the steam from the liquid turned to sweat-like drops. The rest of his face, and his neck, made visible by his collarless white shirt, were curiously pale. He wore no hat. He was a miner to trade.

The fisherman was still squatting before the waning fire when the estate keeper suddenly strode into the clearing in the pines. Without speaking, he halted on the far side of the ashes, his spaniel close behind. Two red, slanting lines crossed his right shoulder across which his shotgun lay.

The fisherman had emptied his can. At his feet lay the tapped-out tea-leaves, gently steaming; and he had lit a cigarette. He glanced once at the keeper, then back to the fire again, filling his dark eyes with the rosy embers, the fading sunset of the blaze now settling to a dull glow.

The keeper, tall, thin, and silent, stood several yards away, mutely accosting the fisherman, radiating black threats. Mutual hostility crossed the space between the two men in invisible dotted lines. Neither spoke. The spaniel, trembling all over, crouched at the keeper's heels.

Then, oppressed by the stranger's strange scent, the dog began to whine softly. The keeper silenced it with a shout, a raw, authoritative ejaculation directed as much at the fisherman as at the trembling, nervous dog. The fisherman, however, did not flinch. He squatted imperturbably on his heels, quite obviously defying the keeper, his eyes lowered.

Skilled in the tactics of dealing with trespassers, the keeper had unconsciously intended to force the fisherman into making some lame remark. Now he lost his temper. Rage flickered up and down the marrow of his legs. It was he who was forced into speaking first.

'Are you aware that this is private ground?' he asked in sarcastic tones.

His voice was thin and sharp and slightly hoarse too. It cut the air as a rusted razor blade might cut taut string. The air between the two men was drawn out taut.

The fisherman did not answer. He just perceptibly shrugged his shoulders, as if dismissing the question as absurd. A moment later he drew deeply on the last half-inch of his cigarette, sucking the smoke down into his coal dust-darkened lungs. Then he exhaled it with a sullen, nonchalant phoooo!

The keeper stiffened. He glared at the bent head of the fisherman, on which the white scalp could be seen between strands of hair, brushed back.

'This is private ground,' he snapped. 'Do you know that or don't you?'

Again the fisherman shrugged. This time, however, he raised his head and, for a fraction of a second, stared directly at the keeper's face. The keeper winced, for the significance of the glance, its insolent significance, was unmistakable. So far as the fisherman was concerned there was no such thing as private ground.

In fact, the miner, when he had completed his five or six pit-shifts each week, felt free to fish wherever he pleased. He fished only in small burns, but if he had wanted to fish protected rivers he would doubtless have fished those too. Rarely did he happen to meet any official who had the authority to turn him off the water, for he came and went so circumspectly he was seldom noticed. Up and down the country, on private estates as well as on public ground, lay the ashes of his fires.

The keeper was shocked to the core of his instincts by the miner's glance. Faced with such perversity, he had a desire to discharge both barrels of his gun at the small, blue man.

And, hard to believe as it may be, the keeper would have fired the gun had he been sure the shooting could have been made to seem accidental. He regularly shot the shrill blue-jays it was illegal to shoot. He felt no more compassion for the small, blue man than for the small, blue birds; both were trespassers, both were a menace to the estate.

The miner for his part was aware of the threat of the two red lines, the two reflections on silver gun-metal of the dying embers of the fire. He was not afraid, however, for crouching at the bottom of the steep, dark bank, he did not feel alone in face of the threat. The keeper swept his eyes across the clearing. Littered with dead twigs, leaves and pine-cones, the ground was spread with shadows of the summer night. A light mist, only visible at a distance, was rising upwards among the tall, slim trunks.

The fisherman's catch, of a dozen small trout varying in size between quarter and half a pound, was lying to the right of the campfire, in a little heap. The pale bellies of the trout gleamed softly. The keeper saw the fish.

'Those are stolen trout,' he said. 'You realise that?'

The fisherman answered with his habitual shrug, a sullen, half-contemptuous twist of his thickset shoulders. After several seconds had gone by he raised his head and again looked at the keeper.

'Trout belong to no one till they are caught,' he said quietly, uttering a coaldust-ingrained truism, an instinctive rather than conscious thought.

The slim, sinewy body of the keeper vibrated like a fence-wire brushed by a marauding fox. His thin lips curled upwards in a sneer: he, too, had instincts.

'So trout belong to no one till they are caught, don't they!' he muttered.

The perversity of the small, blue man made him itch to shoot. The gun was loaded, it was ready to fire. Only the conscious fear of the inquiry that would follow kept him from pulling the trigger.

'They don't belong to your boss till he has caught them,' said the miner, still quietly. Now he was speaking as a miner, not as a fisherman; he was throwing his coal-black, instinctive axioms into the keeper's livid and furious face.

And, crouching back on his heels, small and thickset and sullen, he seemed to throw off the part of fisherman. Shadowy comrades, phantom comrades of the coalface, all squatting, began to gather around him in silent ranks . . . dispelling the threat of the gun.

The spaniel trembled and whined uncontrollably. Fear gripped the keeper as he sensed sullen silent mass of small dark men. At last, defeated in this contest of instincts, his nerve shattered by the radiations of the miner, he turned and strode away. The spaniel followed, still whining, slinking along at his heels.

Not till he was at the very edge of the wall of trees did the keeper halt, and make a last remark. The trespasser still squatted by the embers, now barely red.

'You'll clear off this ground tonight,' he snapped lamely. And he added: 'I'll be back here in the morning to see you're gone.'

The miner did not take the trouble to reply. He raised his head to stare almost casually at the tall, lean man who passed out of sight among the thick trees closely followed by his dog. He began to whistle softly and tunelessly. He was alone below the dark bank, before the dying fire . . .

Later that night, he went away. The keeper returned in the morning. The clearing was empty. Into the cold, black ashes of the fire he solemnly discharged his gun . . .

The Old Fisherman

The old fisherman was seated five or six empty stools distant. He was tall, and slim, bare-headed and grey-haired, and he wore pointed shoes, drainpipe trousers, a blue fisherman's jersey and a dark blue jacket with thin silver buttons like Scotch threepenny bits glittering down the breast and on the cuffs.

Seated on my own stool, I sipped my beer and looked at him, up the bar, over the rim of my glass. I liked looking at him. Each glance was, as it were, like a salty, visual potato crisp. I envied him his high-necked jersey, which might almost have been knitted from a hank of fishing-line. I admired his silver buttons and his lean, brown, grizzled yet dignified face.

As it happened, the bar remained empty but for the two of us. The barman read his newspaper and only heeded us when we tapped our glasses on the counter for another drink. I was on leave, and I might have gone prowling the small town in search of a more cheerful pub had it not been for the presence of the old salt.

Then at last, as was certain to happen, though I had not thought of it, I stole a glance too many, and our eyes met.

The fisherman nodded at me, and even winked, as if intending to say: 'Come and join me, soldier. Let me stand you a drink.'

I flushed, took my eyes away quickly, and hid them in the depths of my beer. I was conscious of not being, or of being more than, the young khaki-clad conscript I seemed to be. All at once all the Odes and Sonnets thrust in the pockets of my uniform – that of a Private soldier – became red hot. They felt like the secret documents of a spy. I stared fixedly into my pint glass; but too late!

'Drink up there, soldier,' urged the fisherman, and he climbed nimbly aboard the stool beside my own. I hesitated, then did as he ordered. I had no wish to hurt him with the revelation that he was about to stand a poet a drink: I would play my part. I would be what I seemed to be as best I could.

'Ahoy there, barman. Two pints and two whiskies, here!' came the rough, friendly voice of my new companion.

The barman, who wore a white shirt and black bow tie like some rare, Siberian type of butterfly, drifted out of his newspaper to serve the drinks.

My heart sank and, turning, I clutched the old salt's jacket sleeve, tugged at it and urgently, very earnestly, shook my head.

'No, no whisky for me. Thanks all the same, but I never touch it,' I said, knowing there was no point in my protestations.

In consideration of the part I was playing, I did not dare to add that whisky made me ill. Moreover, I was lodging with my innocent and highly respectable old aunt, who supposed I had gone for a walk along the sea-front. But the fisherman imagined I was being bashful. He insisted on treating me to the whisky. I took my hand away from his sleeve.

In it, to my horror, was a thin silver button, while from the sleeve there now hung an empty thread. Surreptitiously, I slid my hand down the side of the stool, looking as I did so at the barman's tie. I opened my fingers. The button rolled away with a slow, majestic motion, tinkling – or as it seemed to me, *clanging* – and traversed the length of the bar. Then it turned back towards my stool.

'Lost something, soldier?' The old salt's honest features were twisted with genuine concern.

'Let it go!' I said, giving an airy wave.

'Cheers then, soldier. All the best!'

And, raising his whisky-glass, the old fisherman swiftly disposed of its contents, smacked his lips, and set it down again. So one tosses the dregs in a teacup down the kitchen sink.

'Cheers,' I echoed, and with a sense of foreboding, I raised my own glass, shut my eyes, drew a deep breath, and took a little sip. Ugh! I seized my pint-glass, hoping to quench the hot, golden whisky-fumes with gulps of the draught beer, delicious and cool.

For several minutes I was absorbed in disposing of the whisky.

The fisherman, growing impatient, drew my attention by lifting his elbow and poking it, all of a sudden, into my ribs.

'Guess how many boats I've got, soldier?' he asked me.

I turned and looked into his eyes. They were bright-blue, and hard with innocence, and without, so far as I could see, any bottoms to them. But at the same time they were not deep.

Four boats, I wondered? Five? Six? I shook my head solemnly. 'Sorry, skipper, can't guess. How many boats *have* you got?'

The old salt lowered his eyes and showed me the tobacco-coloured stumps of his teeth in a mysterious smile. For several seconds he kept me waiting in what *he* supposed was dreadful suspense.

Then he held up two coy fingers. Slim, hard fingers, square at the tips, the nails unbitten and the colour of frosted glass.

I feigned astonishment. '*Two* boats, skipper! You must be joking!'

He threw out his jersey-covered chest like a boastful boy, and he laughed so innocently I was suddenly ashamed. Ashamed at deceiving him, at permitting him to stand *me*, a poet, a drink. I almost confessed to him, and pulled my poems out, but – fortunately – I kept my head. Then I made a confession no less disastrous.

'You know, skipper, I've always liked boats. Yes. And to let you into a secret' – my voice was very earnest – 'I'm going to buy a boat. When I'm out of this lot' – I waved my hand at my uniform – 'I'm going in for lobster-fishing, do you see?'

'Bravo!' replied the fisherman. 'Good boy!'

To show the extent of his approval of my decision, he raised his oar-hard hand and slapped my back. I swayed and clutched at the counter. No sooner had I recovered than I was struck by the thought, or rather, since the feeling was more physical than mental, overcome by the sensation, that I had told a lie to this innocent man.

Was that possible, I asked myself? Bewildered by the whisky I had drunk on top of several pints of beer, I gazed inwards, at my conscience. It was golden – the result, no doubt, of the penetrating alcoholic fumes. Yet it was not all golden: among the gold there was some black.

My lobster-fishing-boat-scheme was one of several I had devised for my civilian future. Pictures of bright red lobsters, rough blue jerseys, and small fishing-craft like shaggy sturdy little mountain-ponies made me like it the best. Moreover, under the twin-influence of the old salt and his whisky, the 'scheme' had come to the fore of my mind . . .

Of course, there was a flaw in the scheme. I saw that now – for the first time. For instance, there was the fact that I did not know anything *practical* about boats: nor was I, a private soldier, in the financial position to buy one . . . In short, it was just because I had spoken so earnestly that I had told the old fisherman a lie. If only I had been dishonest and stuck to the truth!

My companion raised his elbow again, and poked it sharply into my chest. 'See here, soldier. Watch this.' And leaning forward, he pushed his pint-glass to one side, dipped his finger in some slops of beer that lay, glistening, on the counter, and, with that impromptu HB pencil, began to trace a diagram or, it might have been, to create a picture of some kind, holding his breath tensely, and curling his tongue.

Curved lines. Straight lines. Relieved that the lobster-theme had been abandoned, and anxious to make amends to the old man, I watched the growth of the work carefully. His shoulder, where it pressed lightly but firmly on my own shoulder, aroused the sensation of a faint, white star. His childlike concentration as he drew made me sad, and, to add to my sadness, some of the liquid lines began to evaporate, and to prove ephemeral, while those that did not invisibly ascend to the ceiling, did not seem to me to make sense. Surely, I thought, he is not creating an *abstract* work of art?

At last, he leaned back, sighed, expelled his breath, drew his tongue in, and raised his bushy eyebrows first at his creation, then at me.

'What is it?' I was forced to ask him.

'A lobster-pot,' he replied.

And so it was; I saw that now! Gripped by a warm, matey impulse, I, too, leaned forward. I dipped my finger in the slops of beer. I made a few quick strokes. I leaned back. At once, horrified at my over-hasty action, I felt my cheeks grow hot, and I hung my head.

I had drawn a lobster, flippant and smiling, in the act of crawling into his serious pot.

I stared at the floor in embarrassment. I only looked up when roars of innocent, deep laughter showed that my act of desecration had been misinterpreted.

'Ahoy there, barman. Two pints and two double-whiskies, here!' shouted the seemingly delighted old fisherman. I shook my head. Promptly the drinks were served and paid for. I had no alternative but to drink up.

'To the lobsters,' I proposed as a toast. 'Cheers,' and I disposed of my whisky at a single gulp and only two hasty sips.

The old salt then looked at me seriously and asked, 'Where do you stay?'

'Stay? Me?' I stammered stupidly. 'How do you mean?'

I raised my pint-glass – my new, freshly-filled pint-glass – and made of its contents what I sensed to be a sinister, dark mask without eyeholes. In its shelter, I asked myself: Dare I tell him? Is he a snob? But I had no way of avoiding his question.

'I am staying with my aunt at 7 Cecil Crescent,' I said, lowering my voice to a whisper as I gave her sedate address.

Foolishly I added, 'I don't suppose you know it very well?'

'Cecil Crescent!' exclaimed the fisherman. 'Why man, I ken it fine!'

I was relieved to find he was not – as my kind old aunt is – a snob.

'I'll be round there in the morning,' he continued. 'Show you how we make the lobster-pots, see?'

I did see: and he must have noticed my expression.

'Don't worry, soldier,' he assured me. 'I've got a barrow, man. I'll bring all the stuff.'

A barrow, I said to myself! The stuff! Those tarry materials with which lobster-pots are sure to be made! I had a vision of my aunt's luxurious, spotless flat, and, as I emptied my pint-glass, I felt very drunk all at once. I had a strong, glowing, golden sensation of the innocence of everyone, even the barman; while I, I sensed, was jet-black.

'Watch what you're doing with that glass!' he, the barman, innocently ordered. I was wickedly holding it up like a telescope and gazing down it at the old fisherman. Simultaneously, I was desperately trying to decide whose innocence – the fisherman's or my aunt's – I was going to betray. Watched by the barman, I lowered my glass. I tucked it under my armpit, telescope-wise.

'How kind of you!' I said to the fisherman. 'You will be round with your barrow . . . about eleven o'clock.'

I could not refuse his kind proposition, so I had made up my mind to betray my aunt. I had already decided, however, that I would send the cushions to be cleaned of the tar at *my* expense . . .

'I'll be there,' said the fisherman, nodding, and speaking in a tone of voice that left no doubt . . . he would . . . be there.

'Now, about this boat of yours,' he continued. 'What size of a boat did you have in mind?'

Size? Boat? 'That's a difficult question,' I answered, truthfully.

'Just tell me roughly,' he prompted.

'Oh, *roughly*.' And after a moment's thought, I held my hands out sideways as if the nose of a salmon was against one palm and its tail against the other palm. 'Say three times that!'

The barman, who was watching my every movement, coughed sceptically, imagining it *was* a salmon.

'Only a little shaggy boat,' I added. 'No funnels.'

'OK, then, soldier,' said the fisherman. 'I'll just take a note of your home address and when I've found a boat for you, I'll send you a letter.'

He dipped his hand into his patch-pocket, produced an old envelope and the stub of a pencil, and, in large, round writing, copied out my home address. Then he folded the envelope into six, spat on it, and tucked it away.

I felt the time had come to make an attempt to explain my real position to the old salt. I perceived, though dimly, that I was about to plunge myself into debt for the rest of my life. 'See here, skipper, about this boat . . .' I began. 'The truth is . . . the fact is . . . I haven't much money. Yes. No. The fact is, I haven't *any* money. I'm penniless, completely broke!'

To make it perfectly clear that I could not afford even a small boat, I felt for my trouser-pockets and wrenched them outside-in. The Odes and Sonnets I had forgotten about were scattered everywhere at our feet.

'My paybook,' I explained. 'I've let it drop.'

Even as I stooped, I heard the voice of the old fisherman raised in protest above my head.

'No money? Don't let *that* worry you, soldier. This is all on me! Barman, ahoy!'

The rest of the story can be told quickly. Though the fisherman did, in fact, know Cecil Crescent, and was kind enough to help me there at the end of our evening, he did not turn up with his barrow the next day. And my leave ended without my seeing him again. But about six months later, when I had left the Army, and was at work on a sheep farm, his promised letter arrived: he had found me a boat.

I opened the letter, read it through once or twice, then sat and gazed at it, miserably. After a time, it seemed that the large, round, open loops of the handwriting were gazing back at me like innocent eyes. I folded the letter so as not to see the loops. Then I tore it slowly, guiltily into little shreds . . .

The Money

At one period in my life, as a result of the poverty I was suffering, it became impossible for me to tell a lie. Consequently, I became the recipient of National Assistance money. But it all began when I applied for Unemployment Benefit money at the little Labour Exchange in the nearest town.

As I entered the building, the typist turned to the clerk and I heard her whisper, 'The artist is here again.' No, she gave me a capital – 'Artist'. The clerk rose, and, making no attempt to attend to me, crossed to the door marked 'Welfare Officer' and gave it a knock.

The clerk was seated. Presently the Welfare Officer appeared. He is, or I should say, was then, a rather stout, unhappy-looking person in his early forties. This afternoon, as if he had known I was coming to see him, he wore a fashionable sports jacket and a large, arty and gaudy tie. My heart went out to him as he advanced towards the counter saying: 'I've told you before. We have no jobs for you. You are simply wasting our time.'

Somehow, I had got myself into a ridiculous, *lolling* position, with my elbows on the counter and my hand supporting my chin. I gazed up at the Welfare Officer and replied timidly, 'I haven't come about a job. I have *been* in a job. Now I have come to ask you for Unemployment Benefit money.'

As I spoke, I could not help glancing at the large, locked safe that stood in the far corner of the room. Out of it, distinctly, a curious silence trickled, rather as smoke trickles out of the stove in my cottage. I had no doubt it was the silence of The Money I had just referred to.

'What!' exclaimed the Welfare Officer, raising his black, bushy eyebrows. 'You have been in a job!'

I nodded. 'I was editing a magazine.'

'And may I ask what salary you received?' he said, his tone disguising the question as an official one.

'One pound, three and sixpence,' I answered, for, as I explained, I could not tell a lie.

'Per month?' he suggested.

'Per week,' I replied with dignity. 'And it was only a part-time job.'

'Hum! In that case, *assuming* that you have been in part-time employment and did not leave it of your own accord you will be entitled to claim part-time Unemployment Benefit money from this Labour Exchange,' he informed me, all in one breath.

'What? But that isn't fair!' I retorted. My cheeks crimsoned; I took my elbows off the counter and waved my hands. 'That isn't just! I paid *full-time* National Insurance money. So I should draw *full-time* Unemployment Benefit money from this Labour Exchange!'

My impassioned outburst brought a nervous titter from the typist and an astonished rustle from the young clerk. The Welfare Officer, however, only glanced at me for an instant, turned his back on me, strode into his office and shut the door.

I waited a few moments. Then, 'Do you think I have offended him?' I asked the clerk. 'Am I supposed to go away now? Do you know?'

But before I had received an answer to my unhappy question, the Welfare Officer appeared once more, bearing two large volumes – no, *tomes*, in his arms. CRASH! He dropped the tomes on the counter, right under my nose.

Then he opened one of the tomes; and slowly, silently, with brows sternly knitted, he began to thumb his way through the thick and closely printed sheets. Page 100 . . . Page 250 . . . And he still had the second of the tomes in reserve.

I moistened my lips, and said weakly, 'Very well, I give in. I am only entitled to draw part-time Unemployment money from this Labour Exchange.'

'That is correct,' observed the Welfare Officer. Closing the tome, and flexing his muscles, he bent to push it aside. Then he took a step or two towards the safe. That, at least, was my impression. Looking back on the incident, I see that he was really going to the cupboard to fetch forms.

But the sight of his too-broad figure retreating to fetch me The Money touched my heart. True, he had won a hollow victory, but I did not mind, and I wanted him to know I did not mind.

'Thank you,' I said, in low, sincere tones.

The Welfare Officer stopped at once. He turned to face me again. 'Thank you? Why are you saying thank you? You haven't got the money yet, you know,' he warned me.

'I know that,' I said, and I apologised to him. He appeared to accept my apology, and, turning, took another step or two towards the cupboard – or, as *I* thought, the safe.

Again I was touched. It was the combination of my poverty, his pathetic appearance in his rich clothes, and the thought of The Money he was about to give me. It was as if he was generously giving it to me out of his own pocket, I felt.

'But honestly,' I sighed, 'I'm awfully grateful to you. You see, if you give me The Money, I'll be able to work . . . I'll be free to work – at last!'

'Work? What work?' exclaimed the Welfare Officer. He halted, flew into a rage, and once more turned to face me. 'If you are going to be working you cannot claim Unemployment Benefit money! Don't you understand that!' he shouted.

At this moment, the typist intervened, saying, 'He doesn't mean work. What he means is, taking pictures. Like that one – I forget his name – who cut off his ear.'

I, too, flew into a rage, and not only at this mention of *ears*.

'*Taking* pictures? *Taking* pictures? *Painting* pictures if you don't mind!' I fixed the typist with my eye, and as a sort of reflex action, she bent forward and typed several letters on her machine. Then, looking at the Welfare Officer, I asked: 'Just tell me, yes, do tell me, how is a person to work when they are in a job? I can only work when I am *not* in a job! When I am in a job I *cannot* work, do you understand?'

'Are you working or are you not working?' shouted the exasperated Welfare Officer at the very top of his voice. 'Think it over will you, and let me know!'

So I thought it over, and that very night, by the light of my oil lamp, I wrote a polite letter to the authorities in the Labour Exchange. In effect, what I said was: 'I resign.' And the following morning, I handed the letter to the postman when he delivered the bills at my mountain-cottage.

But in the afternoon, when I was painting in my kitchen, I happened to look through the window, and I saw a neat little man. Clothed in a pin-striped office-suit and clasping a briefcase, he was clinging rather breathlessly to the fence. Several sheep had ceased to crop the hillside and were gazing at him with evident surprise.

As he did not look like a shepherd, I at once concluded that he must be – could only be – an art-dealer. Overjoyed, I thrust my hairless brushes back in their jam-pot, threw the door open, and ran out into the warm summer sunshine to make him welcome.

My collie dog, swinging the shaggy pendulum of his tail, and barking furiously, preceded me. 'Don't be afraid!' I shouted to the art-dealer. However, he had already scrambled back over the fence, and was standing, at bay, in the shade of the wood.

Calling the dog off, I opened the gate, and, smiling, advanced to meet him with outstretched hand. 'Good afternoon. I'm very glad to see you,' I said. The art-dealer took my hand, shook it warmly, and replied, 'I am from the National Assistance Board. Good afternoon.'

It was then I noticed he had been holding *forms*. The collie still bounded about us, leaping up on the stranger so as to sniff his interesting office-y smells. 'Fin McCuil,' I ordered, 'you mustn't touch *those*. Bad. Go away, now. Chew your bone instead!'

Then I turned to the National Assistance man, and I explained to him, with many apologies, that I had resigned.

He listened sympathetically, but when I had finished speaking, he came a step nearer to me, placed his arm around my shoulder, and said softly, 'Son, there is no need to feel like that, you are perfectly entitled to take this money.'

He tapped his briefcase. He meant, of course, the National Assistance money.

'But I don't feel *like that*,' I assured him. 'Believe me, I feel grateful . . . I mean, ungrateful . . . bringing you all this way . . . But I have resigned . . . I don't think I fit in very well, you see . . .'

'Son,' said the National Assistance man, speaking as no art-dealer ever did, 'I understand your position. No, don't look surprised. I do understand it. For you see, my own brother is a violinist . . .' And breaking off for a moment, he gazed thoughtfully down the steep and rickety old path up to my house. Here was a green, ferny landing; there a hole in the bannisters of bracken where a sheep had crashed through. 'He lives in a garret,' he continued. 'He is in the same . . . er . . . position . . . you see, as you are. He sits up there all day playing his violin.'

So there had been a mistake. It was just as I thought, and almost as bad as if I had told a lie. 'But I don't play the violin,' I pointed out. 'I don't play anything. You see, there's been a mistake.'

'No, no, I understand. You don't play the violin. You paint pictures,' said the National Assistance man soothingly. 'By the way,' he added, 'what do you do with them?'

'Do with them?' I repeated, at a loss. 'Ah, do with them: I see. Well, the big ones I put upstairs, in the attic. The little ones I put downstairs, in the cupboard.'

'You don't ever think of selling them?' he asked gently.

'Selling them! *Ha, Ha!* No, I don't,' I said, delighted by the fantasy of the question.

There was a pause. Suddenly he looked me straight in the eye, and he asked me, point-blank, 'Son, do you want this money?'

I could not tell a lie. 'I do,' I said.

So he thrust his hand into his briefcase. He offered me The Money, and, without looking at It, I put It in my pocket as fast as I could. Money is a great embarrassment when you are poor.

'Just fill those in,' he explained.

So, I thought to myself, they are not pound notes; they are postal-orders. But when we had shaken hands and said good-bye to each other, I found they were not postal-orders, either; they were forms . . .

And I filled them in. And thereafter, till my truthfulness got me into fresh trouble (for, of course, I had been brought up to look on charity as trouble) they sent me a regular weekly cheque. For my part, I was requested to fill in a form stating what Employment I had undertaken during the week and how much money I had earned by it. As painting was not Employment, though it was

Work, I very carefully wrote the words 'None' and 'Nil' in the appropriate columns. After five or six weeks they gave me a seven-shilling rise.

Then I sold a picture. And I was inspected at the same time by an unfamiliar National Assistance man.

It was a breezy, blue and golden day in early autumn when he arrived at the door of my cottage. No sooner had I answered his knock than he cheerfully apologised. 'Sorry, old chap. Can't wait long today. Two ladies down in the car . . .'

'I expect you are going out for a picnic,' I observed, wondering if I ought or ought not to return his wink.

'Ha, ha, old boy, you are quite right there!' he answered.

'Well, do come in for just a moment,' I said. 'I shan't keep you, I promise.'

Lifting my easel out of the way, and hastily removing my wet palette from a chair, I invited him into my kitchen, and he sat down. On my palette, as it happened. He had sat on the chair on to which I had removed it; I at once ran for the turpentine and the cloth.

When we had cleaned him up, I put in tentatively: 'There is something I wanted to ask you. It's, er . . . it's about those . . . er . . . forms . . .'

'Forms?' His bright face clouded over. I was spoiling his picnic with my Prussian Blue paint and my silly questions.

'Those . . . er . . . weekly forms that you send me . . .'

'Oh, those. You mean that you complete those, do you?' He seemed astonished that I did.

But I could not tell a lie. 'I'm afraid I do,' I confessed. 'Do you think it matters very much?'

'Ah, well, no harm done, I suppose.'

'Then there is a difficulty,' I announced. And quickly, so as not to keep the ladies waiting, I mentioned the awful problem I was now faced with. Painting, I explained, was not Employment, though it was *Work*. And even if I stretched a point and called it Employment, still it was not employment undertaken *this week*. The picture I had sold had been painted a whole year ago . . . How was I to inform them of the money I had received for it?

'I want to be quite truthful, you see,' I added. 'The form applies only to the present week . . . So, you see, it is difficult to be truthful.'

'If you want my advice, old boy, *be* truthful,' he answered. 'Yes, be truthful, that is always best. Or nearly always best, eh? *Ha, Ha!* Ah, hmm . . .' He rose, and moved to the door. 'I say,' he whispered to me, 'do I smell of turpentine?'

I sniffed at him, and assured him that he did not. 'The very best of luck then, old chap.' We shook hands. Halting to wave to me at frequent intervals, he hurried down the path, and I returned to the house.

There and then, determined to be truthful at all costs, I set about filling in my weekly form. 'Employment Undertaken – None.' And under 'Money Earned' I carefully wrote – '£5/5/0.' It had, I reflected, that slight suggestion of paradox one expects with the truth.

I posted the form, and, by return of post, I was sternly summoned to the central office of the National Assistance Board.

When I entered the building, and gave my name at the desk, I was at once led, like a very special sort of person, down several long passages and into a room. There, I was awaited. Several men, all of whom, it was plain, were awaiting me, were seated rather grimly around a table. On the table lay my form. Strange to say, it looked completely different there; *absurd*.

On my arriving in the room, one of the men – their spokesman or perhaps the head one – pointed to my form, and said, 'What is *that?*'

'That? Why, it's my weekly form,' I replied.

'Can you explain it to us?' another asked me.

'Yes, easily,' I answered. And I proceeded to explain it to them. Time. Money. Work. Truth. When I had completed my explanation, one of them got up from his chair and fetched a tome. It was a signal, for, at this, they all left their chairs and fetched back tomes. They threw them open on the table.

I grew nervous. After a while, I looked at the one who had first addressed me, and, pointing to his tome, I said, 'You are wasting your time. *I am not in it.*' He looked at me, but he did not smile or reply.

'Gentlemen –,' I began, interrupting them. 'Gentlemen, I think it would be best if I gave up The Money. I don't quite fit in, I quite see that. I sympathise with you. So I resign.'

At this, there was a sudden and very noticeable change in the atmosphere. They were obviously relieved at my decision. They smiled at me. But one of them said: 'There is no need to be hasty.' And another added: 'We wish you well.'

'Then I am to go on taking The Money, am I?' I asked.

But once more there was a change in the atmosphere. The men became grim again, and put on frowns.

'I see,' I said. 'Then I have no alternative but to resign.'

Smiles. Relief. Opening of silver cigarette-cases. 'There is no need to be hasty.' 'We wish you well.'

'I believe you,' I assured them. 'Will you send on the forms or shall I just fill them in now?'

'Now!' said the men, speaking all at once.

So I completed the forms of resignation, and I left the building a free man.

The Boy and the Guess

FOR EDWARD AND KULGIN

It was a fine, sunny, summer day. I suddenly decided I would go for a walk to the end of the rocks. They ran in parallel rows, like railway platforms, from the foot of the blue-shadowed cliffs right into the middle of the bay. On the top of the cliffs was the old town with its grey, ruined spires and bright red roofs, all shining in the sun. The tide was full-out.

I kept on to the very end of the row of rocks, and there a boy was already seated, dangling his bare toes over the calm water. He was one of those immemorial young boys with a thick, blue, hand-knitted jersey and bare, thin, brown legs caked with the white salt from the sea. As I came up, he turned his head, and he glanced at me lazily out of half-open eyes, as though the eyelashes, too, were caked with salt and were too sore to open wider.

'When I came down these rocks,' he said in a slow, thin, drawling voice, 'I had brown hair, but now it's been turned yellow by the sun.'

I looked at his hair but, of course, it was still brown. Then I looked out across the water to where a fishing-boat with a rough, red-brown canvas sail, and with glass net-floats as green as grass-hopper's eyes stacked by the wheel-house, was drifting very slowly around the point of the long rocks next to our own. Then, all at once, there came a puff of wind; the boat's sail filled out, and, with two sort of hops and a glide, it was gone. It was hidden by the rocks. A puff of black smoke from the helmsman's clay-pipe came drifting back towards us across the bay.

'Do you know any riddles?' I asked the boy, as I took a seat on the rock.

He gazed down past his toes to where, on the bottom of the sea, amid the mysterious, dark seaweed, beyond the ledge of our own rock, there was a patch of bright yellow sand.

'No,' he answered after a moment, shaking his toes in a sleepy negative way so that the salt or perhaps the sand-grains between them cracked a little, 'I don't think I do. But do you know any?' he asked.

'I just thought of one,' I said. 'At least, it's maybe not a real riddle that rhymes. It's more, I think, what you'd call a guess – a thing that you've to guess from my hints.'

'Give it to me, then,' said the boy. And, nodding his toes rather doubtfully, he added: 'But you'll have to give me big hints.'

'Then here's a big hint to start with,' I said. 'This thing – that you've to guess – it's like a pony in this way, it is tied up with a rope when it is not in use. In fact, you often see several of them tied up together, in a certain quiet place, and then they are like a string of sturdy little hill ponies hobbled there, tied together nose-to-tail, and all, as it were, nibbling at the grass below a high dyke.'

As I ended the hint, another puff of wind brought the faint tinkling of the sand-donkeys' harness-bells and the shouts of the children who were having rides. They were hidden from us behind the curve of the cliffs.

'Well, did you get it yet?' I asked him.

His toes made polite, thoughtful movements. Half of his mind was on the guess, and half was still on the sand-patch, which was about a yard square, while the water was at least a dozen feet deep. The tide, by then, was on the turn, too. At any moment a big, bearded codfish might cross the sand, like a tiger in a clearing in the jungle.

'No,' he said, 'I didn't get it yet. I think you'll have to give me a bigger hint.'

'Then this thing is like a pony in another way,' I went on. 'I don't mean in its moral character, though they may have that in common as well. No, it's like a pony in this way, that if you were standing on a high rock and then this thing came slowly ambling underneath the rock, like a pony might, you would get an awful itch in your toes. You would start to wiggle your toes and then, suddenly, with a yell like that of a cossack or of a wild, drunken tinker, you would take a flying jump down. Down, you see, onto this thing. Now have you got it?' I asked.

'No, I still haven't got it,' said the boy. 'You might see a big fish down there,' he added, pointing with one big toe at the sand-patch.

'Then think of a caravan, instead,' I said. 'Not one of those horrible, streamlined, modern caravans, but one of the old kind with a door made in two halves, so you can keep the bottom half shut, to lean your elbows on, while the top half is still open and you can gaze out . . .'

'What would you see?' he asked me.

I scratched the salt-grains in my yellow hair. 'What would you see? Well, you'd see the sad, blue smoke from your own chimney, and . . . and then some thin little trees . . . crooked trees with the loch behind. And then, of course, you'd see your horse. Yes. Your poor old horse tied up to a tree with a long bit of rope that would rustle in the grass when he shook his head.'

'Got it!' exclaimed the boy, his toes twitching with excitement, 'it's a horse!'

'Silly,' I said, 'it is not a horse.'

'But it was you yourself said it was tied up with a rope,' he protested.

'All the same, it isn't a horse.' I said. 'And besides, the horse is irrelevant. It's the old caravan we're concerned with. For this thing – that you haven't guessed yet – is like a caravan in this way, it is very exciting to go inside it. Just as it's nicer in a caravan than in a house, so this is more exciting than a caravan. Only you go down into it instead of up.'

'Has it wheels?' asked the boy.

'No,' I said, 'it hasn't wheels. It has – oh, better than wheels.'

'Wings?'

'No, better. Better even than wings. And you would probably have to bend down while you were inside, and you might be offered a big mug of tea. Boiling hot, black tea with condensed milk.'

'No,' said the boy, now shaking his toes quite despondently, 'no, I'll never get it. It's too hard. But then,' he added, 'I'm only thirteen.'

And just with that, the same fishing-boat came drifting slowly back around the point of the next rocks. There was a sudden puff of wind, and the rough, red-brown canvas sail filled out. Then the boat came gliding smoothly right under the lee of our own rock. The boy was on his feet in an instant. He began to wiggle his toes and then, suddenly, with a wild, delirious, ringing yell, he leaped down on the deck. There came a second puff of wind, and the boat skipped away out to the open sea. I sat on there, watching the sand-patch, wondering if a big, bearded cod-fish would swim in with the tide. Sometimes I could hear the sand-donkeys' bells.

Straw

My father kept an impoverished clothes shop in the city but we both hated it with all our hearts. What we wanted was a little place in the Highlands, up in the hills somewhere, and with a burn close by the house. One of those burns with white waterfalls, pools of a brownish colour, ferns and rocks.

It was my father's firm opinion that there are a lot of little burns scattered over Scotland which have never been fished. And it was one of these that we hoped for – the trout so innocent we could not but catch them; and neither of us able to fall asleep at night for the noise of their rises splashing the burn-water on our window and walls.

So, every night, as soon as we had cleared the supper dishes from the table, we would spread out the day's newspaper and search in the advertisement columns for a suitable place. It was agreed between us that we weren't interested in any property of over five hundred acres, or with a salmon river within its bounds. But when we saw a smallish place that seemed to suit us, my father would take his fountain-pen and mark the advertisement with a cross. (I remember how the two blue strokes of the cross always blotted on the coarse newspaper.) And then – so we felt – it was ours: *our place*.

Once in a long while my father would shut the shop for the day, and we would take a bus into the country, in the hope of finding one of those burns. I remember the last day we did that, for it was only about a month afterwards that my father took ill very suddenly, and died.

. . . Late – as we always were – we boarded the tram for the bus-station. And then, just as though it were a further part of our own slowness and lateness, we were held up by an accident. A horse had fallen in the street. Over the shoulders of the crowd, I could see the horse, and the carter, who was placing straw under its head. 'More corned beef!' said a fat fellow-passenger in a jocular voice; and I was pleased that my father didn't join in the laugh that followed.

. . . At last we alighted from the bus. It was the middle of the afternoon by then. We were laden heavily with all the fishing-gear which my father had insisted we might possibly need. Slowly we made our way across a meadow towards a burn we had noticed as we sat in the bus. I ran on ahead of my father to take a look at the pools.

'Keep back there, my boy!' he shouted. 'I believe there is someone fishing in that pool already.'

Sure enough, the fisher's flies flew into sight, and the line, as it uncurled, made an 'S' shape over the low bushes. I hurried on to the next pool, upstream, but only to find that it was occupied too. There were already fishers in all of the pools, so there was nothing else for it but to turn back to the road.

But, the road was three fields distant by then. My father looked anxiously now at his gold watch, and now at the sun, which was quite low in the sky. We reached the road and began to trudge down it, and when we had walked for what seemed a very long distance – about five or ten miles it felt – we came to a hump-backed bridge. My father stopped in the middle of the bridge, and pushed his hat further off his brow.

'Yes,' he said, gazing over the parapet, 'this looks to me like the sort of burn that will never have been fished.'

So then we began to climb up the hillside. And when we had found a bit of the bank that was not too steep, we slithered down it to the edge of the burn. The water – it was very white and cool-looking – rushed over the stones into a fine wide pool. But the red beams of the setting sun had begun to slant through the solemn black pine trees that grew at the water's edge, and I was impatient that we should start to fish.

'Yes, my boy,' said my father once more, as he searched in the creel for the special, Woolworth's tin-cup from which he always drank of the pure burn-water. 'I am positive this burn has never been fished. Those little trout there will never have seen a wet-fly.'

It was at that very instant that I myself saw a wet-fly, one of an old, snapped-off cast hooked in a pine branch that hung over the water. While my father continued the search for his tin-cup, I passed the time in retrieving the cast.

'A drink of water, my boy?'

My father had found the cup and was about to drink from it – always a solemn moment for him.

'No thank you, father,' I replied, rather coldly, for the sight of the sunset reflected on the silver sides of the cup was distressing to me. 'I think we ought to start to fish soon,' I ventured to say.

'The younger generation,' he replied, 'is always rushing. You ought to take a drink of God's pure burn-water while you have the chance.' He threw his head back impressively, and took a small sip from the cup. Then he flung the rest of the water across the dry stones where it made a long dark splash.

We set up the fishing-rod. Then it only remained to choose a fly-cast and to tie it on to the line. As soon as all was ready I hurried down the river-bank to the pool below. My father did not believe in casting (he called it 'unnatural') so he would just draw a long length of line from the reel, and then throw the flies into the water. I would let him know where they had floated, and if the fish were rising to them.

'Ready down there, my boy?' he shouted. I could see his eager, anxious figure in the distance, the white water mounting up in waves around his black waders as he prepared to throw out the flies.

'Ready here!' I shouted up.

The reel made a rusty, hoarse kind of noise, then nothing happened for a while. Then all of a sudden the three flies appeared in the pool down below me; but they were preceded by the line, which had somehow got into a great knot. The several small trout I had been watching slid over the pool with an unpleasant, hand-in-pocket sort of air. They permitted each of the flies to float past, and all the while as they were squinting at them in that furtive way, they slightly shuffled their pointed fins. It seemed to me that they were *whistling*, too.

'Any rises yet?' enquired my father in a voice filled with hope.

'Not exactly,' I answered, for I hadn't the heart to inform him of the great fankle in the line.

The next thing that happened was, the fankle suddenly unwound itself, and the flies were swept down the pool. In an instant they were carried out the tail-end of it, and into the rapids beyond. I could see them jumping up and down there, and I knew there would be a whole series of little plucks, just like rises, going back up the line to the fishing-rod, and of course to my father's hand as well.

'The Evening Rise!' he shouted excitedly. 'Stand back, my boy! I am going to strike!' (He seldom struck; it was 'unnatural'.)

He struck, and there was a splash in the rapids, and a shower of spray and of pine-needles; and then the sound of a wood-pigeon flying out of the top of the pine tree above my head.

'Will you be able to climb that tree?' said my father, wading slowly towards me with an expression of disappointment on his face.

I shinned up the tree and rescued the flies. They were water-logged by then, so they had to be dried out. My father made a dozen or so false casts, the fishing-rod gripped in both hands, like a garden-spade; while there was a sound from the line as though a whip were being cracked. By then, there wasn't a fish to be seen in the pool, so it scarcely mattered that the flies weren't on the line when it next came down. And soon the chill in the air, and gathering shadows, made us hurry down to the roadside to catch the bus for home.

'You know,' said my father when once we were seated, 'I am inclined to the opinion that someone had been fishing that little burn. It seemed to me that someone had been scaring those trout.'

I was far too sleepy to answer. In fact, we both fell asleep. We staggered out of the bus-station and onto the tram. Where the horse had been in the morning, there was only an empty bit of road, lit by street-lamp, and in at the edge of the pavement lay a few straws which were lifted and whirled as we rocked by. We puffed up the tenement stairs to the door of our house.

My father made for our supper the dish that he always made when we'd been out fishing: the end of a ham and a cabbage boiled up in the same pot. And as soon as we had cleared the dishes from the table, we spread the newspaper on it, and began to search the advertisement columns for a place just as we did on an ordinary night.

'You know,' said my father, looking up from the newspaper for a moment, 'you ought to have tried a drink of that burn-water. It was the most delicious drink I have tasted in years. Now this place here,' he went on – 'it would suit us fine, don't you agree?'

He read the advertisement aloud, to see if the place had my approval, taking up his fountain-pen as he did.

'Goodness me!' – he said – 'there's sure to be a little burn near a place like that. Why, my boy, in all probability there'll be a little burn that has never been fished – not once – not ever since God said: "Let there be light;", and there was light on the pools. Not too much light, though,' he added. 'Too much light is bad for fishing.'

Suddenly, then, I pictured the pools: the light on the little brown pools, and on the ferns and the rocks. And for a reason I failed to see at the time, I saw the carter placing straw under the head of the poor horse. Tears came into my eyes.

'Oh Daddy, there *will* be!' I said. 'There's sure to be a burn like that! Why, we'll never sleep a wink all night for the rises of the trout!'

My father took a firm hold of his fountain-pen and marked the advertisement with a cross.

Pills

The doctor was about to leave the patient. Standing in the open door of the bedroom, he patiently repeated the instructions which he had already given to her three times. He wanted to make quite sure that she understood what she was to do.

The doctor was a small, neat, handsome man with dark hair, a dark moustache, a suit of a soft brown colour that seemed to echo his personality, white gloves, and dark brown, pointed shoes. He stood with the shoes set close together, leaning slightly forward as he spoke. In one hand was his black medical bag, and in the other, almost as noticeable, was his cross – the cross of long hours, hard work, and of patients who, as this one, would not trouble to follow his advice.

It was a beautiful, blue, summer afternoon. Through the wide-open window of the bedroom (it was the doctor himself who had opened the window), came the droning of a distant farm-tractor, and, more loudly, the rustling caused by the prehistoric, yellow toes of the hens as they scratched along the bottom of the black-tarred shed just beyond the sill.

The bedroom was a fairly large room, but it was sparsely furnished, and such furniture as there was in it had the look of having just been flitted in, or else of being just about to be flitted out. There were two straight-backed chairs and one armchair, the double-bed, and a small bedside table on which there stood a bottle of medicine, a tea-cup, a copy of *The People's Friend*, a dessertspoon, and a small box of pills.

'Now,' said the doctor in his soft, slow, 'brown' voice, 'you are on no account to rise from your bed – on no account, do you hear?

And you are to take the medicine three times a day, as I already explained to you, and two – two,' he repeated, 'of the heart-pills, once.' He paused, and looked across at the patient's face to make sure that she was taking in what he said.

She was a small, plump woman, with swollen cheeks and eyelids, and bed-tousled hair. She lay to the extreme far side of the bed, so that the other three-quarters of it seemed to be left to the phantom of her husband, the shepherd, who was up on the hill just now, 'looking' his sheep. The green eiderdown quilt was drawn up to her nostrils, and in her eyes, which were fixed on the ceiling, was the expression in a rabbit's eyes when it is crouching among rushes to wait till you have gone by. The doctor was the only middle-class person who came into her household, and she always felt uncomfortable as long as he was there. She wished he would hurry and finish his speech.

'Well, I think that's all,' he said, still in his 'brown' voice, behind which came the strange, pale rustles of the yard straws disturbed by the hens' scratching toes. 'The District Nurse will look in tomorrow to see how you are.' He paused again, and smiled sweetly, while he swung his black medical bag to and fro, and, as it were, took a firmer hold of his cross. 'Now, look after yourself. Take the treatment, and remember, on no account are you to get out of bed. Call me at once,' he added, 'if you have another turn.'

He nodded, and, still smiling sweetly, gently closed the door of the bedroom. His neat footsteps went down the lobby, and into the kitchen, from which another door led through to the scullery, and then out into the yard where he had parked his car.

Och that Nurse! thought the woman, her face now showing the first signs of interest. That meant she would have to start and scrub the kitchen floor. The Nurse would expect to find the place looking spotless when she called. She lay thinking of the Nurse with the same sort of awe as people once thought of the Minister. Indeed, she pictured the Nurse as a sort of female minister, very stern, and clad in dark colours, and always on the look-out, not for Sin, but – it was the same thing – for Filth.

She lay still for a few moments longer, and then, sitting up in bed, she looked to see the colour of the new pills the doctor had brought. This time they were only brown; sometimes they were of a brighter, more cheerful colour. In either case, she did not take them, because, as she had learned from experience, they made her giddy and short of breath while she hurried about doing her housework.

She lay down again, still thinking of the District Nurse, and listening with impatience for the doctor's car to drive out of the yard and down the lane.

While passing through the kitchen on his way to the car, the doctor stopped for a moment, and, with his shoes set close together, gave a quick glance around the room to see if it was tidy. He was pleased by what he saw, but as his inspection was an instinctive one, it did not strike him to ask himself how the kitchen came to be in such a clean state.

It, too, was a fairly large room. The ceiling was high, and there were two tall, broad windows. Both of these, however, were filled to the very top with the shadow of the hill. Under one of the windows was the table, covered with oilcloth, and bare except for one teacup, a teaspoon, and a few small crumbs. There was a big, old sofa in front of the grate, and the fire, which had been banked up with dross, had just burned through, and cast red reflections on the shiny, brown wallpaper. To each side of the grate stood an armchair. In one of the chairs slept some cats; they were rolled up into a ball and it was impossible to say how many there were. In the other slept an old collie dog who, as soon as he saw the doctor, sat up with a low growl. Then he jumped down, and slunk between the doctor and the chest of drawers, along the far wall, and in below the table. Four eyes, two of which were merely his round, brown eyebrows, peered out.

The doctor was just about to go on into the yard when suddenly a deeper shadow crossed both windows. There was the sharp clatter of hobnailed boots on the stone floor of the scullery, and then the shepherd strode into the kitchen. Seeing the doctor, he stopped at once. While still out in the yard, he had taken off his cap, and had meant to toss it across the room, and on to the top of the chest of drawers. Now he let the raised hand with the cap in it fall to his side. Except for one, short 'Aye', he stood and stared at the doctor without a word.

The shepherd was a very tall, very lean man. He had close-cropped, red hair, high cheekbones, and narrow, grey eyes; and he wore a royal-blue canvas jacket with short, narrow sleeves that left bare his knobbly wrists, that looked like two, shiny, winter apples. And he also wore a pair of narrow, black trousers, and big boots laced up with knotted string.

'Ah, I'm glad I bumped into you,' said the doctor with a sweet smile. 'I was wanting to have a little chat with you about your wife.'

At the word 'wife', the shepherd seemed to grow even more silent, and he looked out of the window.

The doctor waited to be invited to sit down, and then at length, seeing that he was not to be invited, he gave a sweet, broad smile, and, crossing to the sofa, he sat down of his own accord.

The sofa, as has been said, was an old one. It had hardly any of an interior left now, and it was only sat on, or rather, in, by the dogs and cats of the household, and maybe in the springtime, an odd lamb.

When the doctor sat on it, he fell into it as far as the waist. Then, smiling still more sweetly, he balanced himself on the very edge of it, and, setting his black medical bag down on the floor, he laid his cross, as it were, on his knees, which were set close together as he sat.

'Wouldn't you like to sit down while we have our little chat?' he asked the shepherd. He nodded at the armchair which had been left empty by the old dog.

The shepherd hestitated for a few moments, then he dropped his cap back on his head. After hesitating for another few moments, he crossed the kitchen and did sit down, on a straight-backed kitchen chair, in the far corner, behind the sofa. The corner was deeply shadowed by the hill.

Cautiously, the doctor turned his head around. All he could see of the shepherd was a long, lean shadow, and four highlights, two of which were on the knees of his trousers, while two were on his wrists.

'Well now,' he began in his soft, 'brown' voice, 'what I wanted to say to you was . . .'

Whee Whee Whee

A sudden, loud squealing interrupted the doctor's little chat. Breaking off, he looked questioningly at the shepherd, because the squealing did not come from the yard outside, but was there, in the kitchen. It seemed to come from the chest of drawers.

The shepherd, who was seated bolt upright and motionless in his dark corner, briefly explained:

'It's the pig.'

'The pig?' The doctor was sure it could not really be a pig in the chest of drawers. He felt a little shocked at the idea, and said:

'Now we are joking. Surely not?'

'Aye, aye, man,' said the shepherd in a matter-of-fact, slightly impatient voice, as if he secretly thought the doctor a bit slow, 'it's the pig.'

Sure enough, the bottom drawer of the chest of drawers stood a little open. And in the drawer, in a cardboard box, with a sucking bottle in its mouth, was a little pig, pink, with pale blue markings on the back as though it had been tattooed. It had drunk all the milk in the bottle, and, besides, its hot water bottle had grown cold now, so it had begun to call out.

The shepherd got up, crossed the floor, and closed the drawer with his boot-heel. The squealing grew more faint. He sat down again, this time on the kitchen chair that was now nearest to him, in the other corner of the room. It was even more in the shadow of the hill. The doctor rose from the sofa, and, very cautiously, sat down facing the other way, and tried to make out the shepherd. 'Well,' he began again, with a sweet, if strained, smile, 'well . . .'

But there was a second interruption in the chat. Now a sweet little girl with wide eyes, and a big, blue bow in her red hair, had come slowly wandering into the room, humming to herself. She carried her schoolbag and her pet rabbit, a white rabbit with long whiskers and black spots. As soon as she saw the doctor, she screamed, and somehow the rabbit fell to the floor, and it began to hop around the sofa chased by the growling old dog.

. . . At last, when the little girl, the old dog, and the pet rabbit had all run outside, the doctor made a new start with the little chat. 'All I really want to say is, your wife must on no account get out of her bed. If she doesn't rest and take the treatment . . .' He left the sentence unfinished, and rose, and, picking up his cross and his black medical bag, he walked towards the door of the scullery. On the way there, feeling that there was something rather strange about it, he paused to inspect a potted plant that stood on the window-ledge.

In fact, all the blossoms had been snipped off the plant, and the leaves cut down, to make it look more tidy. Rather the same sort of thing had happened to the cherry tree out in the yard. You could still see its stump.

The doctor, still puzzled by the strange plant, straightened, turned to the shepherd's corner, forced a smile, and said, 'Good afternoon.'

He left the house.

Presently, the car drove out of the yard and away down the lane. When the dark sound of the engine had at last faded into the distance, the shepherd got up from his chair in the corner. He poked his head out into the lobby, and as he hurled his cap on to the chest of drawers, he shouted:

'Wife? – Are you there wife? Where's the tea?'

'Coming, coming!' came the reply from the bedroom.

And the woman soon came through to the kitchen in her stocking-soles. She filled the kettle and set it on the fire; then she roared the fire to heat the water. She wanted the kitchen to be perfectly Pure when the Nurse called in the next day.

A Broken Engagement

When I was young and we had our money – we lost it afterwards we kept a maid. That is, we kept several one after another, but I remember only one of them, the maid Peggy, a plump, grown-up girl with rowanberry-red cheeks, black hair, a white apron, and a black dress . . .

Our house was two-storied, and Peggy must have had a bedroom in it, but the kitchen was really more her place. I mean 'her place' in the nice sense: the place you would normally go to look for her, and where, in the evening when the work was finished, she was free to amuse herself just as I was in the drawing-room, upstairs. The kitchen was downstairs, in the basement. This was just under ground level and was reached by a flight of old-fashioned, steep stone stairs which were lit by a gas-lamp even by day.

I used to go down there a lot in the evening, after tea. At that hour, with the several straight-backed chairs tidied, the table newly scrubbed, and the day's dishes and pots and pans washed and laid by, there was a feeling in there like that of a sunset – a beautiful, still, sad sunset when the birch and pine trees, even the brackens, are so very, very still it is as if they have been bewitched . . . Just such a feeling was over the chairs, the dewy table, the neatly stacked dishes and the shining pots and pans that hung in a row from the same shelf.

'Peggy?' I would say as I came in. 'Peggy? – Peggy draw me a face.'

She might be seated in front of the big kitchen range which, being now closed and banked-up for the evening, was – in this indoor sunset – the equivalent of that faraway, bright rosy band above the woods. Or else she might be seated, hands propping her chin, at the table, bent over a love-story magazine, a weekly magazine printed on a coarse, off-white sort of paper and with illustrations in black line.

Almost certainly she would agree to draw me a face. And, in practice, that meant several faces, copied either from the illustrations to the love-stories in the magazine or from those to the advertisements (for corsets, cheap scent, and so on) that appeared on the pages towards the back. She would stand up, and crossing to the shelf beneath that for the dishes, she would fetch the writing-pad, the pencil and india rubber; then, having carefully sharpened the pencil to a fine point with the old kitchen-knife, she would begin to draw me a face . . .

How can I say how lovely it was? I would lean up close to her, my elbows on the table, scarcely breathing – breathing very slowly through my open mouth while I held my tongue curled up just as if there was some mysterious, radar connection between the carefulness of the moving pencil-point, and *its* . . . Then, after a while, a sort of painless pins-and-needles would start to creep up me, beginning, I think, in about the knees; and after another while I was half-asleep . . . As for the face Peggy drew, it was one with long, literally shiny eyelashes, two dots for nostrils, smiling rose-bud lips, and bobbed hair. (This I pictured as being of a brown colour.) And, as soon as one face was completed, 'Now draw me another, Peggy,' I would say. Because I couldn't bear that she should stop drawing and so break the magical spell . . .

One night I met my mother at the head of the stairs down to the basement. She said, 'You're not to go down to see Peggy tonight.'

'Oh, but Mummy,' I protested, 'why can't I?'

'Never mind! Why should you, a child, be told why you can't? You just aren't to go down; that's all.'

I turned and went into the drawing-room, but later, my mother having for some reason gone up to her bedroom, I did go downstairs.

Everything in the sunset kitchen was just as usual, except that an unfamiliar, grown-up young man was seated on a kitchen chair, opposite Peggy, to one side of the range. He was seated very upright and very silent; and he wore a blue suit and had a red face and hands which, spread out stiffly on his blue knees, were exactly the colour of Lifebuoy soap. What was *he* doing here? I thought: And as he, it seemed to me, was ignoring Peggy, I decided to ignore him, too.

'Peggy?' I said. 'Peggy? Peggy, draw me a face.'

Imagine my astonishment when she shook her head and said, 'No. No faces tonight. Just you be a good little boy and run away back upstairs.'

And the young man, suddenly taking his eyes, as it were, from that rosy band above the woods, said, 'Go on, sonny. Listen. There's your Mummy calling you. Now run along.'

That, of course, was untrue, but I went. I left the two of them alone there, silent, their straight-backed chairs like two separate rocks. I wondered if they really were as bored as they seemed.

And after that the young man came into the kitchen in the evening quite often. Harry something was his name. Once he had a thick bandage across two fingers of his right hand. Peggy said he had hurt it at his work. He always sat very upright and very silent, and then he pretended to hear my mother calling on me from somewhere upstairs. One night when he wasn't there I noticed that Peggy was wearing a new ring . . .

'What's that?' I asked her.

I spoke softly, but even so I broke the magical spell that lay on us as we sat drawing faces out of the love-story magazine.

'That?' said Peggy. 'That's a ring.'

'Yes, I know,' I said. 'But what's it for, that ring?'

'It's an engagement ring,' she said.

'An engagement ring – what's that?'

'It means I'm going to be married.'

'Now?'

'Soon.'

'To Harry?'

'Yes, to Harry.'

'Oh. Now draw me another face. You've spoiled that face,' I said.

And the young man, Harry, came more, and then still more often, so that we never drew faces. I have the impression that he was in the kitchen – Peggy's kitchen – every night. And a long time, maybe four or five whole weeks, passed. The bad time had an end one night when, as I came into the kitchen expecting to see Harry there, I found Peggy all alone and, as I thought, fast asleep. Her arms were folded across the love-story magazine, which wasn't open, and her head was laid on her arms.

'Peggy? Peggy?' I said shaking her by the shoulder. 'Peggy, draw me a face.'

After all, she wasn't asleep, but she didn't look up then – only shook her head once or twice.

'Oh go on,' I pleaded. 'Be a pal. Just one face.'

'No, please,' She shook her head again, several times. 'Please no faces tonight.'

'Oh *please*, Peggy. Please. Just one. If you do –,' I hesitated, 'if you do you'll be my best pal, for life.'

So Peggy stood up, and she went through the beautiful, still, sad sunset to fetch the drawing things from the shelf. Her eyes were swollen and red round the edges as though, maybe, she had been crying: and as she stood sharpening the pencil with the old kitchen-knife I could see a red mark on her finger where she had had the ring. Then she opened the love-story magazine and began to draw me a face. I leaned up close to her, scarcely breathing; the painless pins-and-needles crept slowly up me. It was lovely! . . . Soon I was half-asleep.

The Potato Field

Autumn. All down the potato field, from the top fence down to the slightly hazed fence away at the bottom, stretched a wavering, would-be straight line of pickers – women, and little boys, and girls; a broken-down breakwater stretching into a cold, calm, misted sea . . . The females wore heavy boots and brightly coloured head-squares; almost every little boy seemed to have had the loan of his big brother's cast-off jacket for the day. Between the sudden swoops made down the field by the Digger, they sat resting on their wire baskets, then, as the noisily rattling machine swooped yet again, they scrambled up, bent, and, like desperate human scare-crows, began to grab at the golden, gleaming vegetable-nuggets that were left scattered thickly on the top of the earth.

As fast as they could, red, frost-nipped hands tossed the potatoes into the baskets, and these in turn were emptied into a cart. It was drawn by a tractor, and had rubber pneumatic tyres on its wheels which bumped on the muddy ruts as it went slowly along. At the cart's tailboard trudged a young worker who was new to the place. It was his job to deal with the full baskets, and when he had hoisted each up, and slung it, empty, back to the picker, he gave the driver of the tractor, with whom he was not on speaking terms, a curt nod.

The driver, an old man, had been fully thirty years there. Perhaps because he had been so accustomed to horses he had a strange style of driving. At a first casual glance he was seated there as if in the saddle of some dangerous stallion; but at a second glance it was really more as if he was in church – in church, and seated, on his hard Scotch Presbyterian pew, under the eyes of the minister, *and* God's . . . For he sat up very straight, stiffly straight, and whenever he leaned forward to work a gear it was just as if that gear was some familiar text – 'An eye for an eye', perhaps – some familiar Old Testament text which he *ought* to have been able to lay his hand on immediately, but which, perversely, had a way of eluding him at first . . . And then, having found the gear, and worked it, he would sit up very straight again, and he would look all about him with the guilty sense of being *watched* . . .

When at length the cart had collected a full load of potatoes it swayed off to the pits. There were two of these so far, two long, narrow, low mounds, made of straw and earth, standing towards the top of the field. And a third pit was now almost half-built. Two grown men worked there, one, a neighbouring farmer, shovelled the earth on, the other shaping the potatoes as they were tipped from the cart, and sometimes helping to add the straw. The straw glowed yellow in the blue, dim October light. And the low-set, long pits suggested Viking ships – Viking ships that were sailing, as the earth was, into the mystical, Northern months now ahead.

Also, a little over from the pits, and nearly at the top of the field, was a bonfire, consuming the dried-up potato stems. It was stoked by a young teenage boy. He, in the heat of the flames, had flung his jacket off, and his shirt-sleeves were rolled into hard, white knobs up his arms. The fire crackled loudly in the autumnal silence; the smoke from the orange flames rolled in curves down to the pine-woods, where it spread out into a thin haze . . .

Finally, at the very top of the potato field, in a central position, was the man in charge. He was not the foreman – there was no foreman on that farm; and neither was he the farmer, for he, who had pneumonia, was not present in the field. No, he was just an ordinary worker elevated to a position of full authority, and responsibility. So he kept a specially careful watch on the work. Sometimes, too, he glanced across at the farmhouse, at one of the upper bedroom windows which was darkened by a drawn blind.

The farmer, as he lay there in the twilight, in the clean white sick-bed, had long ceased trying to see through the blind and out to the field. Instead now he concentrated on the sounds from the field. And from these he was able to build up a picture, an accurate picture of the progress of the work. There were the sudden swoops that the Digger made, the stray autumn-vivid shouts of the little boy and girl pickers ... the crackling of the bonfire ... the intermittent droning of the old man's tractor ... and over all, like a sort of dark, bare, twisted thorn bush, the ceaseless cawing of a flock of crows.

A smile was on the farmer's pale, sick face. Then, as the minutes passed and still the Digger did not make another swoop, the smile slowly died away. He began to frown and tried to struggle from the bed.

In fact, the Digger now stood halted at the top of the field. Something had gone wrong with the important part for unearthing the potatoes. The driver, a spanner in his hand, leaned over it, tapped the propeller-like blades, and scratched his head. The man in charge looked across at him anxiously. And all down the field the weary pickers, seeing the likelihood of a lovely, long stoppage, had begun to settle down on their baskets; while the pale hush crept into the field. Shouts rose up like hurled caps or dark clods. Only the crows kept cawing, the bonfire crackled, and the old man's tractor droned evenly as it reversed slowly down near the bottom of the fence.

And why was it reversing? Well, there was no practical reason for its doing so. There was, however, a moral reason. The old man, seated there stiffly upright, and carried slowly backward, the potato-laden cart lurching behind him, was teaching the young new man a lesson in – he was not quite sure what. Anyway, it was a much-needed moral lesson. And, knowing roughly where the fence lay, he did not have to glance around – was able to keep his eye fixed on the other who now stood about halfway up the field.

He was in a wretched state of mind. Unconsciously, he had picked up an old earth-ingrained sack and was nervously twisting it into a knot in his hands. For he was aware of several baskets that were now full of potatoes, and if those baskets were not emptied before the Digger was repaired and made another swoop . . . Then the pickers would have nowhere to put their potatoes; but the thought of such a happening was almost too terrible for him to frame . . . And there was nothing, *nothing* he could do but to stand there awaiting the return of the cart.

And the cart simply went on reversing, the old man with the outward air of one engaged in some elaborate, mysterious but also absolutely necessary manoeuvre. 'Youth,' he thought to himself. 'Depravity – God – Twenty milkmaids – Thirty gardeners.' These last, the milkmaids and gardeners, were, of course, a memory from *thirty* years before, and, as the young new man had been employed there for no more than the past fortnight, they were somehow a proof of his being depraved. 'Three farm managers. Five hundred fine Friesian cows.' So the moral lesson went on. Meanwhile, unnoticed, the wheels of the cart had struck a rut. As they did, they had jumped, and had come down at an angle, and were now turning the wrong way. That is, the laden cart was slewing out behind the tractor. And when it had slewed out a little farther it would certainly jam the tractor, and would probably throw it on its side. The old man might be crushed beneath it . . . killed.

The man in charge looked towards the darkened window in the farmhouse. 'Unfaithful servant; thou hast let the Digger break down.' He imagined the accusing voice of his employer. He even half expected to see his pale face appear against the blind. Then he set off towards the Digger to discover if he could assist the driver with the repair. And it was then that he saw the slewing cart. The slewing of the cart *and* its probable consequences. He saw the tractor toppled, the old man lying crushed underneath it, he himself descending the stairs from the sick bedroom – sacked. He prepared to avert the disaster – to rush dramatically down the field shouting, 'Stop! Stop! You'll be killed!' But, to his astonishment, he found that his legs, the marrow of which seemed to be frozen, would not obey him, nor would his tongue.

And the new man, too, saw the slow slewing of the cart, together with its probable consequences. He was immediately filled with joy. Ceasing to twist the old sack, he prepared to wait passively, joyfully, for the accident. For it seemed to him that the tractor, in the moment when it threw the old man down, and crushed him, would actually be the hand of God crushing him, punishing him for his sins. Especially for the sin of having tried to order *him* – the young new man – about the place. But then, to his astonishment, his instinctive, animal nature suddenly rose up. It overwhelmed his moral nature, and, in spite of all he had learned as a boy in Sunday school, he dropped the sack to free his arms, gave a warning wave, and shouted: 'Stop!' As the old sack fell, it covered his boots, and he had a funny appearance of being buried up to the ankles in the field.

In the pale hush the shout rang out distinctly. It was heard by the pickers, who raised their heads, while those who were both near enough and sufficiently intelligent saw both the slewing of the cart and, as had the other two, its probable consequences. But even so, they continued to watch without much concern. For they were either young or were female, and as the cart and tractor formed a part of what they thought of as the 'Men's work', it was not for *them* to interfere. That would be sinful. So they simply looked on as if across a moral gulf.

And the old man himself heard the warning shout. At first, however, he felt sure that he could not have heard it, for even *he* had never imagined the young new man so depraved, so disrespectful of his elders, as to publicly order *him* to 'Stop'. Then he realised that he really had heard the shout, and he had a vivid picture, not only of the thirty gardeners and twenty milkmaids, the three farm-managers and five hundred fine Friesian cows, but also, and especially, of the wonderful way the thirty gardeners would run and hide in the bushes whenever the Lady of the Big House appeared for a walk. They would run into the bushes and hide there, scarcely breathing, and certainly not keeking, till she had passed out of sight. And yet the new man had shouted: 'Stop.' 'By God!' he thought. 'By God!' And he leaned forward to work a gear, not the gear that would stop the tractor, and so save him, but the gear that would cause it to reverse – *Zoo-ooom!* – at the speed of a jet-plane, so he imagined it, down the field.

'STOP!'

This time the shout was from the top of the field. It was the voice of the man in charge. Seeing the old man lean forward, and assuming that he was about to work the gear that would stop the tractor, he had recovered the use of his frozen faculties. And he now dashed forward melodramatically, flying down the long line of astonished pickers, while, in a loud, authoritative voice, he shouted: 'Stop! Stop the tractor! You'll be killed!' Then, when he had sprinted almost to where the young new man was standing, he lost his breath and had to slow to a walking pace. They fell in side by side. Together they began to walk the rest of the way down the field.

For, behold, the tractor had stopped.

The old man had worked the wrong gear.

Instead, as it were, of 'An eye for an eye', he had laid his hand on 'Love your neighbour'.

Now he sat up very straight again, and as he began to look about him guiltily he suddenly found that he *was watched*. The young new man and the man in charge – both, he saw, were watching him; and for some reason, too, they were laughing together, laughing, and waving behind him, at the cart. Suspecting some sinister reason for the laughter, the old man decided to join in. Thereby he would neutralise it, and he might even be able to steal it and turn it against his enemy.

All three of them laughed uproariously, and the laughter soon spread across the field to the pickers – they were so bored they were glad to laugh. It spread up the long line of pickers, and it presently reached as far as the two grown men at the pits. They, too, joined in. And finally it spread even to the lone boy at the bonfire. Great gusts of laughter rose from the field, and when the sound had reached to where the crows flew, they soared with a sudden, fierce cawing, which was like a black laughter, and almost brushed the clouds with their ragged wings . . . Then the Digger, repaired now, made another swoop . . . In the nick of time, no more, the young new man swung up a full basket . . . The pickers scrambled up . . . Bent . . . Began to grab at the golden, gleaming vegetable nuggets . . . The farmer lay back . . . and laughed.

PLAYS

THE ESTATE HUNTERS

Only the samovar hummed drearily,
and everything was the same as before.

(From a Russian novel)

CHARACTERS

Mr Farquharson

John

Two Fishers

SCENE ONE

A kitchen in a tenement. A summer evening. Through the window are the jumbled roofs of other tenements, shipyard cranes and factory chimneys. MR FARQUHARSON, *age sixty, sits at the table, while his small son* JOHN *makes a pot of tea.*

MR FARQUHARSON: Is that tea ready, my boy?

JOHN: Yes, father. Almost.

MR FARQUHARSON: And is it strong?

JOHN: Yes.

MR FARQUHARSON: Black?

JOHN: Yes.

MR FARQUHARSON: How many spoons did you put in the teapot?

JOHN: Four. One for me, one for you, one for the pot – and one extra.

MR FARQUHARSON: Put another spoon in for me, my boy. And let me have that newspaper, will you—.

JOHN: Here you are. [*Takes the newspaper from below the cushion on the armchair, and passes it*]

MR FARQUHARSON: Thank you, my boy. And now my fountain pen . . .

JOHN: Where is the pen?

MR FARQUHARSON [*jokes*]: How should I know? Just look around for it, it can't have vanished. It must be *somewhere* . . .

JOHN [*opens a drawer. Finds the pen*]: It was in the drawer beside the spare fishing-tackle.

MR FARQUHARSON: Thank you. Splendid. Then there's only one last thing . . .

JOHN: What?

MR FARQUHARSON: My spectacles.

JOHN: Your—. But you've got them *on*!

MR FARQUHARSON: Well, so I have. And I never noticed. [*Pause.*] All right my boy, you can pour the tea now. No. Wait.

[JOHN *looks at his father.*]

You're quite sure you didn't forget to let it stew for a couple of minutes?

JOHN: No.

MR FARQUHARSON: And it's nice and black for me, is it?

JOHN: Yes. It's like tar.

MR FARQUHARSON: Good. Splendid. Then you can go ahead and pour it out.

JOHN: I'm *trying* to . . .

MR FARQUHARSON [*looking*]: What—?

JOHN: I'm trying to pour it. It won't pour . . .

MR FARQUHARSON: That sounds to me like *very* good tea, my boy.

JOHN [*pokes with his finger in the teapot*]: I made a mistake with the number of spoons, I think. I think I must have put *four* spoons in the teapot *twice*.

MR FARQUHARSON [*thoughtfully*]: Plus one extra . . . makes nine spoons . . .

JOHN: I think so. About that . . .

MR FARQUHARSON [*pretends to be cross*]: 'About that' – what do you mean, my boy? And you expect to be a fisher—. You want to grow up and be a big boy, and catch a lot of trout – and you can't even count the spoons –. [*He shakes his head*]

JOHN: It's all right now. It was only the spout of the teapot was choked with tea-leaves.

MR FARQUHARSON: Well, I don't wonder.

JOHN: But what we *ought* to have is a proper mustard tin.

MR FARQUHARSON: A mustard tin—. What for, my boy?

JOHN: To put the tea in the pot with. A mustard tin instead of a teaspoon. Haven't you noticed – all the fishers put the tea, and the sugar, in their billycans from a mustard tin.

MR FARQUHARSON: But not when they're at home, in their own houses, I shouldn't expect.

JOHN: They make good tea . . .

MR FARQUHARSON: Well, we might try it. See you remind me to bring a tin of mustard up with me from the shop tomorrow. I have some in stock.

JOHN: But you aren't *going* to the shop tomorrow.

MR FARQUHARSON: Well, that's so. I'd forgotten. But neither I am.

JOHN [*anxious*]: You didn't forget we're going into the country for the whole day tomorrow, fishing?

MR FARQUHARSON: No, I certainly didn't forget. [*Pause*] We'll just have to make do without the mustard.

JOHN [*puzzled*]: The . . . mustard?

MR FARQUHARSON: Well, there you are. And you think *I* have a bad memory. . . . Didn't you just ask me to bring you a tin of mustard home from the shop?

JOHN: Oh, father—. Really. Don't you see, it isn't the mustard we want – it's *the tin.*

MR FARQUHARSON: Oh, is it—. Well, that reminds me . . .

JOHN: What?

MR FARQUHARSON: I knew there was something I was meaning to ask you. It's been in my head ever since I came in here. And now I remember. It's my tin cup. Did you remember to pack my tin cup for tomorrow? When you're out in the country you get thirsty, and then there's nothing in this world even half as good as a drink of water from some little burn.

JOHN: Well, the tin cup's packed. And here's your tea. [*He pours it out and sets it on the table*]

MR FARQUHARSON: Thank you, my boy. Thank you. All we need now is my fountain-pen . . .

JOHN [*sighs*]: I passed it to you already. It's there – see? – under your saucer. [*Pause*] Are there many 'For Sale' advertisements in the paper tonight?

MR FARQUHARSON [*looks in the newspaper*]: Well, let's see . . . yes. Yes, there are. . . . There are one . . . two . . . three . . . four whole columns.

JOHN: Then what's the first place that's for sale. Read it out.

MR FARQUHARSON: Don't rush me, my boy.

JOHN: I'm not rushing you.

MR FARQUHARSON: Yes, you are. Don't argue with your father. The younger generation is always rushing. [*Pause*] Was that clock wound last night? What's the time?

JOHN [*looks at the alarm-clock on the mantelpiece*]: Ten past eight.

MR FARQUHARSON [*taken aback*]: Oh, is it—. Already. Still, we have practically the whole of the evening to go through these advertisements. Bring a chair in here by me.

JOHN: All right. [*He puts a chair in at the table, kneels on it chin-in-hand, and waits*]
[*After a pause*] Aren't you going to read out the first advertisement?

MR FARQUHARSON In just a minute, my boy. Don't rush me. . . . You can't just rush into a thing of this sort. It takes time. It may even take *years*.

JOHN: I don't think we'll ever find a place that suits us . . .

MR FARQUHARSON: Of course we will. Are you ready now? Are you listening?

JOHN: Yes . . .

MR FARQUHARSON: Then I want you to listen very carefully, and tell me if this first place is a place we would want to buy.

JOHN: Yes, yes. I know that.

MR FARQUHARSON: Well, here's what it says. [*Reads*] 'For sale. Stately country mansion. Thirty bedrooms. Dining rooms. Lounges. Maids' accommodation. Etc., etc. Plus 2,000 acres. Pheasant, grouse shooting. Salmon fishing. Trout.' [*A long pause*] Well?

JOHN [*uncertain*]: We *don't* want to buy it . . .?

MR FARQUHARSON: My boy, I am asking *you*. I don't have to tell you that there are only the two of us. So it's up to you, too, to say what you think.

JOHN: How big is 2,000 acres?

MR FARQUHARSON: How big—. Well, let's see . . . you know that back-green down there below the window?

JOHN: Yes.

MR FARQUHARSON: Well, try to think of the back-green, *including* the dustbins, and then multiply it – well, 4,000 times.

JOHN: Whew—!

MR FARQUHARSON: What do you say?

JOHN: I think we don't want to buy it. I think it would be too big for us.

MR FARQUHARSON: Well, there you are, you see. That's just what I think too. As a matter of fact, we couldn't buy it. A place like that would be – pretty expensive. But of course that's no reason for us not to give it our careful *thought*. [*Pause*] And so you agree it's not a place for us to buy?

JOHN: No. Yes, I mean. What's the next place?

MR FARQUHARSON: Don't rush me . . .

JOHN: I'm not rushing you . . .

MR FARQUHARSON [*continues*]: And even if we *could* afford to buy it, I may say I wouldn't want to. I have never had any inclination to fish for salmon. What about you?

JOHN: No, I haven't either, I think.

MR FARQUHARSON: And besides, there's another point that's just occurred to me. Neither of our rods would hold a salmon. So – where's that fountain pen got to? – I'll just score it out. [*Does*] There—. My boy?

JOHN: Yes . . .

MR FARQUHARSON: Speaking of rods . . .

JOHN: They're both rubbed with oil and all ready for tomorrow.

MR FARQUHARSON: Well, that's splendid. I'm glad to hear it. But – speaking of rods – what I want to say is, are you absolutely positive you didn't forget to pack my tin cup?

JOHN: No, I didn't forget. Everything's packed.

MR FARQUHARSON: We're all prepared to set off first thing?

JOHN: Yes.

MR FARQUHARSON: I know one thing you *did* forget to pack, though.

JOHN: No, I didn't . . .

MR FARQUHARSON: Yes, you did.

JOHN: What?

MR FARQUHARSON: Those new wet-flies.

JOHN: Well, I didn't. They're packed too. Everything's packed. The new wet-flies, and your tin cup, and the dry-flies, and the minnow, and – and the old wet-flies, and a hook in case we want to use the worm.

MR FARQUHARSON [*horrified*]: What—?

JOHN [*hesitant*]: I put in a hook in case we want to use the worm . . .

MR FARQUHARSON: Where did you get it?— You didn't *buy* it?

JOHN: No . . .

MR FARQUHARSON: Well, what then?

JOHN: I found it . . .

MR FARQUHARSON: Where? Not in *this* house—.

JOHN: No. Stuck in the branch of a tree. When we last went fishing. It was stuck in a branch over the water, and that was how I knew it couldn't be – like *you* said it was – a little burn that had never been fished.

MR FARQUHARSON: My boy, I did not say that burn was a little burn that had never been fished. I only said – when we first got there –

that it *might* have been a little burn that had never been fished.

JOHN: But it had been fished, though, because I found the lost hook stuck in the branch.

MR FARQUHARSON: Well, I could see that for myself. Just as soon as we'd started fishing, I could see we weren't the first ones who had fished for those trout. Not by a long way . . .

JOHN: They wouldn't look at our flies at all . . .

MR FARQUHARSON: Well, that's so. I don't deny it. But – do you want us to descend to using *a worm*, my boy? What sort of fishers do you think we are?

[*An awkward silence. There is no answer*]
Eh?

JOHN [*wistfully*]: It would be nice if we could catch a trout . . .

MR FARQUHARSON: My boy, to listen to you saying that, anyone would think we had *never* caught a trout . . .

JOHN: But it would be nice if we could catch *another* trout . . .

MR FARQUHARSON: Well, and why shouldn't we?

JOHN: I don't know . . .

MR FARQUHARSON: Well, there you are. [*Pause. Then for the thousandth time*] My boy, it's my opinion that there are a lot of little burns scattered up and down this country that have never, ever, been fished.

JOHN: Yes . . .

MR FARQUHARSON: Yes. So they are sure to be *full* of the most innocent little trout.

JOHN: Yes . . . I suppose so . . .

MR FARQUHARSON: You suppose so? But my boy, I am telling you. Those burns will be simply *seething* with trout that have never, ever, so much as *seen* a wet-fly.

JOHN: But what if they know it's the *wrong* fly?

MR FARQUHARSON: Those little trout –. Don't talk such rubbish. How could they know it's the wrong fly? When they're so innocent – when they have never been fished for – just *any* fly would be the right fly for *them*.

JOHN: You really think we'd catch one?

MR FARQUHARSON: One . . .? One . . .? You're a pessimist. We'll catch dozens.

JOHN: When?

MR FARQUHARSON [*drawn up*]: Well, er, tomorrow . . .

JOHN: But suppose we can't find that sort of burn? Suppose it's just like last time? Last time we couldn't find even *a pool* where there wasn't someone fishing before we got there. We were late in getting away. All you kept saying was, 'Don't rush me.' And we just walked and walked and walked, and you made us carry all that heavy tackle, and by the time we got started and set the rod up, it was time to come away.

MR FARQUHARSON: Well, that's so. I have to admit it. But – well, the place we went to last time wasn't lonely enough. That was all . . .

JOHN: Yes. But we had to go just where the bus went.

MR FARQUHARSON: Well, just you wait till we get ourselves a car. As soon as we can afford it, we'll buy ourselves a little car, and—.

JOHN [*interrupts*]: But tomorrow we won't have a car.

MR FARQUHARSON: No. Tomorrow we won't. . . . But still . . .

JOHN: What?

MR FARQUHARSON: Well, but still. . . . But still we may catch a trout . . .

JOHN: Oh, I don't think we'll ever find a burn that has never been fished. *Or* a place that suits us . . .

[*Music. The light starts to dim*]

MR FARQUHARSON: What. . . . Don't talk such rubbish. Of course we'll find a burn. *And* a place. Our needs are very modest. All we want is a little cottage. – A little country cottage, with oil-lamps – and of course with a burn that's not too far. A little burn that has probably never been fished. So the trout will all rise like mad, and – and they'll splash the water right up on our window, and . . . and we'll not be able to sleep – we'll not get a wink of sleep – the whole night. But it won't matter if we don't sleep because there'll be no shop to go hurrying down to. There'll be no shop – and no tenements. Just the hills and the trees all around us – and the little burn . . .

SCENE TWO

The same. The following morning. Bright sunlight. JOHN *looks out of the* *window.* MR FARQUHARSON *stands by the table which is absurdly strewn* *with rods and creels.*

MR FARQUHARSON: Now let's see. . . . Have we got everything? The two rods. . . . [*Lifts them*] Yes. And both creels. . . . Yes. And you're quite positive you packed my tin cup? It would be a disaster if we were to go off without it. Just suppose we got thirsty. . . . Suppose we were wanting a drink of the burn water and then we found we had left it behind? Eh? [*Pause*] What's the time on that clock, my boy?

JOHN [*turns*]: It's almost ten.

MR FARQUHARSON: What—. And we've been up since six. That clock must be wrong. It's unbelievable how the time flies. What are you doing, standing there at that window—. You ought to be helping me to pack.

JOHN: There's been an accident.

MR FARQUHARSON: What—. What sort of an accident? Is it serious?

JOHN: It's a coal-horse. It's fallen down in the street.

MR FARQUHARSON: And can't they help it up again?

JOHN: No. I don't think so.

MR FARQUHARSON: Why not?

JOHN: It's an old horse, I think. At least it looks like an old horse. And there's a big crowd standing around it. They must be going to shoot it soon, I expect.

MR FARQUHARSON: Well, that's a shame.

JOHN: Yes, isn't it—. Oh. Here's a policeman . . .

MR FARQUHARSON: What?

JOHN: A policeman. He's just come. He's got out his notebook and he's speaking to the coalman. No. No, that can't be the coalman. . . . That's the coalman there, that's kneeling—.

MR FARQUHARSON: What?

JOHN: That's the coalman that's kneeling, putting straw under the horse's head. And stroking its nose. He's making it comfortable till they come and shoot it. And—.

[*The doorbell suddenly jangles*]

MR FARQUHARSON: Goodness. There's the postman. That clock must be right after all. . . . Go on, my boy – go into the lobby and see what he's brought us. But don't bother me with any bills today. We haven't the time to be bothered with bills.

[JOHN *goes out into the lobby and comes back holding a letter*]

JOHN: There's a letter for you. And it's typed.

MR FARQUHARSON: Is it sealed or unsealed?

JOHN: Sealed.

MR FARQUHARSON: Then find me my spectacles. Be quick. No. Just you open it. But hurry. What does it say?

JOHN [*opens the letter and reads it*]: Oh—.

MR FARQUHARSON: Don't tell me it *is* a bill, after all . . .

JOHN: No. It's from the estate-people.

MR FARQUHARSON: The—. What estate-people? What are you talking about?

JOHN: Don't you remember? The people you wrote to in reply to the advertisement in the paper last week.

MR FARQUHARSON: Oh. Them. Yes. . . . Well, what do they say?

JOHN: They say they're willing to sell you the estate.

MR FARQUHARSON [*very embarrassed*]: Oh, are they—. [*He coughs*] Hmn. Well. . . . Well, we'll see about it later. We simply haven't got the time to think about it now if we're going fishing. Just put the letter away in the drawer – yes – and come and help me check over this stuff.

[JOHN *sighs loudly*]

What?

JOHN: We've checked it already. We've checked it *twice*. We're going to be late again, just like last time. I knew it. We won't find even *a pool* by the time we get there. [*Sighs*] What's the use . . .

MR FARQUHARSON: All right, my boy. We won't check it. We'll go at once. We'll catch a tram.

JOHN: There's no good you saying that *now*.

MR FARQUHARSON: What—?

JOHN: All the trams are held up by the accident.

MR FARQUHARSON: Then – here, catch hold of this rod, my boy – we'll take a bus into the bus-station.

JOHN: All the buses are held up as well, now.

MR FARQUHARSON: The buses too—. That's awkward. But—. Well, we'll just start and walk towards the bus-station. We may get a lift.

[*They begin to pick up the equipment as the curtain slowly comes down*]

SCENE THREE

In the country. Evening of the same day. In the foreground, a burn with a pool; in the background, pine trees and an old stone bridge. The rays of the setting sun slant redly through the pines.

At first, as the curtain rises, it might almost be 'a burn that has never been fished'. But then a fisher, that is, an angler in a working-man's suit and a shirt with no collar, comes down the bank and starts to fish in the pool. After several casts with the wet-fly he hasn't caught anything, and he goes away.

Another fisher comes up to the pool. He also casts, and, at the third or fourth cast, his fly gets caught up in a tree by the water. He tries to disentangle it but finally breaks the cast. Goes away . . .

MR FARQUHARSON *and* JOHN *then appear on the bridge. For a moment they stand silhouetted against the sun's rays. They are absurdly laden with equipment, and are tired, dirty and hot. They have walked for miles and miles.*

MR FARQUHARSON *sits, exhausted, on the rear parapet while* JOHN *comes forward to look into the pool.*

MR FARQUHARSON [*mops his brow with his handkerchief*]: Keep back my boy! Keep back!

JOHN: I *am* keeping back.

MR FARQUHARSON: No, you're not. You're looking. [*Pause*] If I have told you once, I have told you a hundred times, you mustn't show yourself to the trout.

JOHN [*looks over the parapet*]: Maybe there aren't any trout. . . . Oh! Yes, there are! Look! Oh! Here's one.

MR FARQUHARSON [*shouts*]: Don't shout, my boy! Don't shout! You must go up cautiously. They can *hear* as well as *see* . . .

JOHN [*points*]: And there's another! Here's another! Here's another! Oh, come and look at it! Come and look! [*He is beside himself with excitement*]

[MR FARQUHARSON *gets up – it is an effort – and comes forward to the parapet*]

MR FARQUHARSON [*solemnly, after a pause*]: Well, my boy, this looks to me as if it might be a little burn that has never been fished.

JOHN: Then let's *start* fishing.

MR FARQUHARSON: Don't rush me, my boy. Don't rush me . . .

JOHN: I'm not rushing you. I'm not. I'm only saying we ought to start and fish.

MR FARQUHARSON: Well, but now we've found a burn, I really think the best plan would be for us to come back and fish in it some other day. Don't you?

JOHN: No. I don't want to fish some other day. I want to fish *now*. I can't wait. I'll *die* . . .

MR FARQUHARSON: Well, but what about the bus? It's the last one, you know. Suppose we miss it? Eh?

JOHN: We won't miss it. . . . Hurry. You put the rod up and I'll open the creel and get out the flies.

MR FARQUHARSON: All right, my boy. But I want you to do something for me first.

JOHN: What?

MR FARQUHARSON [*solemnly*]: Just a little thing. Unpack my tin cup and go down there and fetch me up a drink of the burn-water.

JOHN: Then you get the flies and set the rod up. Promise?

MR FARQUHARSON: Yes. But go cautiously when you're down there. . . . Don't scare the trout.

[JOHN *comes down to the pool. He fills the cup and passes it over the parapet, to his father.* MR FARQUHARSON *drinks elaborately. Stands the cup on the parapet. Sets up the rod. Meanwhile,* JOHN *discovers first an empty beer bottle, then the fly that was lost in the tree*]

[*As he sets the cup down*] Ah. That was delicious, my boy. Just delicious . . .

JOHN [*as he finds the fly*]: Oh –.

MR FARQUHARSON: What is it?

JOHN: I've found a fly here.

MR FARQUHARSON [*misunderstanding*]: You have—. Well, that's a stroke of luck for us. Now you must try to match it with one of ours, my boy.

JOHN: I don't mean that sort of fly.

MR FARQUHARSON: What?

JOHN: It isn't a real fly, that was flying about. It's a fisher's fly. It was caught in this tree.

MR FARQUHARSON: Caught in the tree—. How do you suppose it got there?

JOHN: I suppose it means this burn *has* been fished.

MR FARQUHARSON: I'm afraid it looks like that, my boy. Still. Still, perhaps it has *almost* never been fished. Eh?

JOHN: Yes. Almost never. . . . Perhaps.

MR FARQUHARSON: But I think we ought to leave it and come back another day, a bit earlier. Don't you?

JOHN: No. I want to fish now. I'm *going* to fish now, even if you aren't. Are you ready?

MR FARQUHARSON: Yes, my boy. I suppose I'm ready . . .

JOHN: Then you stay up there and cast from the bridge, and I'll stay down here and keep watch on the flies in the pool. Right?

MR FARQUHARSON: Very well, my boy. But remember, no shouting. And no dancing about either. You've to behave yourself down there, do you hear?

JOHN: Yes, yes, yes. I know that. But hurry. . . . Hurry . . .

MR FARQUHARSON: Don't rush me, my boy, don't rush me. . . . And don't forget to be listening for that bus.

JOHN: Yes . . .

MR FARQUHARSON: Well, are you ready?

JOHN: Yes. . . . Yes . . .

MR FARQUHARSON [*raises the rod*]: Then here we go . . . [*He casts. That is, he makes half-a-dozen ludicrous practice-casts, the line cracking each time like a circus-whip. Finally he lets the flies simply fall over the parapet*]

JOHN [*jumps about in wild excitement*]: Hurray! Hurray! Hurray!

MR FARQUHARSON [*calls down*]: Contain yourself, my boy. Contain yourself . . .

JOHN: Yes, yes. . . . Yes.

MR FARQUHARSON: Can you see any trout down there now?

JOHN: Thousands.

MR FARQUHARSON: What?

JOHN: Hundreds. . . . Hundreds of trout.

MR FARQUHARSON: Stand still. And don't exaggerate.

JOHN: I'm not. I'm not. There's dozens of trout. Just down there.
[*Points*]

MR FARQUHARSON: Are there—. And do they look innocent?

JOHN: No. . . . Not *very* innocent.

MR FARQUHARSON: And where are the flies? Can you see them yet?

JOHN: Yes, yes, here they're coming now. Drifting down the stream.
But—. Oh dear—. Oh—. Oh dear . . .

MR FARQUHARSON: What? What is it, my boy?

JOHN: It's the flies . . .

MR FARQUHARSON: Well, but what about them?

JOHN: They've hooked on to each other. They're in a great big
fankle.*

MR FARQUHARSON: Are they? Dash it—. Is it a really bad fankle?

JOHN: Yes. No. Sort of . . .

MR FARQUHARSON: Then I'd better just reel them in.

JOHN: No, don't. Don't. Wait just a tick . . .

MR FARQUHARSON: Very well. If you say so. But where are they now?
Can you see where they are?

JOHN: Yes. They're almost up to where the trout are swimming.

MR FARQUHARSON: Any rises?

JOHN: No. Not yet. Oh—.

MR FARQUHARSON: What? Was that a rise then?

JOHN: No. Now the trout are swimming *away* from the flies. [*Pause.
Then, an outburst*] Oh, how I hate them! How I hate them!
They're just like horrible corner boys – only instead of pointed
shoes they have those horrible, ugly pointed fins. And they don't
even *run* away from the flies – they just look sly and sidle off . . .

MR FARQUHARSON: Never mind. I'll reel up and try again, eh?

JOHN: No, wait. Wait just a second. Wait till the flies have gone
right down to the bottom of the pool. *Please*.

MR FARQUHARSON: But what about that bus, my boy?

JOHN: I'm listening for it . . .

* *fankle:* a knot.

MR FARQUHARSON [*excitedly*]: A rise!

JOHN: What?

MR FARQUHARSON: There was a rise! I felt a rise!

JOHN: It's not a rise. It's just the rapids. The flies have gone right down the pool, and now they're in the fast water, and it's plucking at the line. It only *feels* as if it was a rise . . .

MR FARQUHARSON [*absorbed*]: Another rise! A whole lot of rises! It must be the Evening Rise! Stand back!! Stand well back!! I am going to STRIKE!!!

> [*He strikes. The line flies up, and up, and into the tree that stands by the water. A pigeon coos and streaks out*]

MR FARQUHARSON [*flatly, disappointed*]: My boy, do you think you can climb that tree for our flies?

JOHN [*uncertain*]: Yes, I expect so . . .

> [*He goes to the foot of the tree. Looks up to the top of it. A horn blares distantly*]

MR FARQUHARSON: The bus—! There's the bus! The bus is coming now, my boy. Be quick! Be quick!!

> [*There is a moment of panic as the curtain falls*]

SCENE FOUR

The kitchen. Late the same night. A crescent moon shines in the window. MR FARQUHARSON *again sits at the table while* JOHN *makes the tea.*

MR FARQUHARSON [*with forced heartiness*]: Is that tea ready, my boy?

JOHN [*tired and dispirited*]: Yes, father.

MR FARQUHARSON: Thank you. Splendid. Then you can pour it out. [*Pause*] Just wait till tomorrow night—.

JOHN: Tomorrow night—. What for?

MR FARQUHARSON: I'm going to bring you home that mustard tin you wanted.

JOHN: Oh, that—. It doesn't matter . . .

MR FARQUHARSON: What? But of course it matters.

> [JOHN *sets his tea on the table*]

Thank you. [*He notices* JOHN's *face*] Why, my boy, you've got a touch of the sun.

JOHN: What? [*Goes slowly to the window*]

MR FARQUHARSON: You've got the sun on your face today. [*Pause. Sips his tea. Tries to humour* JOHN] Delicious. This tea couldn't be better if it *had* been made with a mustard tin. Now that newspaper – where's it got to?

JOHN: I don't know . . .

MR FARQUHARSON: There it is there. On the cushion on the chair, my boy . . .

[JOHN *hesitates, then passes it. Goes back to stand at the window*]

MR FARQUHARSON: Thank you. . . . You're a good boy. And now you can come and help me.

JOHN: Help you—. What to do?

MR FARQUHARSON: What—. What a funny question. To look for a place for us, of course, my boy. There are a lot of places in tonight's paper. One . . . two . . . three . . . four . . . five whole columns. What do you think of that?

JOHN: I wish . . . [*Breaks off*]

MR FARQUHARSON: Well, what do you wish? Go on.

JOHN: I wish we *had* caught a trout today . . .

MR FARQUHARSON: And so do I. So do I. Still. . . . Still, we almost caught one, didn't we?

JOHN: When?

MR FARQUHARSON: Don't you remember? At the very end. Just before the bus came. When I struck.— And we almost caught a pigeon.

JOHN: That was just the rapids . . .

MR FARQUHARSON: Still. Still, we'll be sure to catch a trout *next* time. Eh?

JOHN: No, we won't . . .

MR FARQUHARSON [*surprised*]: What? What do you say?

JOHN: No, we won't catch a trout next time . . .

MR FARQUHARSON: You're tired, my boy, that's all. You're a wee, sleepy boy. Now come and help me look through these advertisements.

[JOHN *shakes his head slowly*]

MR FARQUHARSON [*looks up from the newspaper*]: What? Aren't you coming to help me?

JOHN: I don't want to do the advertisements.

MR FARQUHARSON: But *I* want you to, my boy. Just suppose that tonight was the very night there was a place that exactly suited us? Suppose there was a little cottage with—.

JOHN [*interrupts in a flat voice*]: There won't be.

MR FARQUHARSON: Eh—. Don't say that. [*Pause*] What are you doing there?

JOHN: Nothing . . .

MR FARQUHARSON: Then come away from that window and sit down here, by me.

[JOHN *shakes his head*]

What are you looking at? What's out there?

JOHN: Nothing . . .

MR FARQUHARSON: Nothing—. Then what are you thinking about?

JOHN: Nothing . . . Yes. Yes, I'm thinking about the horse.

MR FARQUHARSON: The horse—?

JOHN: The horse that had fallen in the street today.

MR FARQUHARSON: Oh. In the morning. I remember. The poor, old coal-horse. It had fallen down in the street. But it can't *still* be there?

JOHN: No. There's only the straw . . .

MR FARQUHARSON [*puzzled*]: Straw?

JOHN [*as if to himself*]: They were laying straw under its head. They were stroking its nose. They were going to shoot it . . .

MR FARQUHARSON: Please, my boy. You'll have me crying in a minute. [*Pause*] If you won't come and sit beside me, at least you'll listen while I read out the first place. You just listen very carefully, and then say exactly what you think.

JOHN [*softly*]: I think it wouldn't suit us . . .

MR FARQUHARSON: What—. But how do you know it wouldn't? Have you read it? Eh?

JOHN: No. But I just *know* . . .

MR FARQUHARSON: But you can't know beforehand. And I think it might be the very place for us.

JOHN [*turns*]: Yes . . .?

MR FARQUHARSON: Yes. It doesn't actually say so, but I expect there'll be a little cottage they would let us have fairly cheaply. And there's sure to be a burn. Don't you think there'll be a burn?

JOHN: Yes . . .

MR FARQUHARSON: Yes, I feel sure there'll be a burn. Why, it'll probably be a burn that has never been fished. Never, my boy – do you understand that? Never. Never . . . Not once. Not ever since God said: 'Let there be light' – and there was light on all its little pools.

JOHN: Yes. On the little, brown pools. On the ferns, too. On the rocks . . .

MR FARQUHARSON: Yes. . . . But not *too* much light, because, if you have too much light, it isn't good for fishing. Did you know that?

JOHN: [*goes slowly up to his father*]: Yes. . . . Too much light isn't good for fishing.

MR FARQUHARSON [*delighted*]: And so you *are* going to help me. . . . Well, that's splendid. . . . This tea is delicious, my boy. Delicious. And tomorrow, we'll get a mustard tin. . . . You really ought to have had a drink of that beautiful burn water. . . . But what am I talking about? Oh, yes. We were going to look through the advertisements. . . . So you do think there'll be a burn?

JOHN: [*with tears in his eyes*]: That has never been fished? Yes, I do. Yes, honestly Daddy, I'm sure there will be . . .

[*Pause. They both face the window. The light in the kitchen starts to dim. Music*]

There'll be a little country cottage – with oil-lamps – that we can afford to buy quite easily. And of course there'll be a burn, too. And it'll never have been fished. Not once. And so the trout – they'll be *so* innocent. . . . All night they'll be rising like mad, and—. Oh, Daddy, Daddy, it will be so wonderful! We'll never – neither of us – sleep a wink all night – not a wink all night – for the rises – of the trout!!

[*The stage is dark. The window throws its golden light on their faces. They are smiling and crying. Slow curtain.*]

WALKING THROUGH SEAWEED

CHARACTERS

First Girl

Second Girl

The scene is a city street of the 1960s, at dusk. Two teenage girls have sauntered up to look in a shop-window. Three doors away is a café with a juke-box, its raucous or wistful pop songs carrying faintly into the street. Music: any wistful pop song.

FIRST GIRL: See them toffee-apples in the window?

SECOND GIRL: Yep.

FIRST GIRL: Real old-fashioned they look.—Fancy toffee-apples . . .

SECOND GIRL: You ever ate toffee-apples?

FIRST GIRL: Yep. Sure we ate them. Lots of times. When I was wee we was great on toffee-apples. But I wouldn't eat one now. It'd be undignified.

SECOND GIRL: Maybe I could go in the shop and get one of them toffee-apples . . .

FIRST GIRL: And eat it now – out here in the street? Not when you're out with *me* you don't eat a toffee-apple . . .

SECOND GIRL: Oh well, all right. . . . But I think it would be nice to have eaten one of them toffee-apples.

FIRST GIRL: It's OK for kids to eat toffee-apples. But we ain't kids now. We're sixteen.

SECOND GIRL: Yep. Grown-up women.

[*Pause. The pop song grows momentarily louder*]

How do you like that one that's on the juke-box in the café now?

FIRST GIRL: I never heard that one before.

SECOND GIRL: It was on the telly.

FIRST GIRL: Was it? When?

SECOND GIRL: Last Sunday.

FIRST GIRL: We ain't got a telly yet.

SECOND GIRL: No.

FIRST GIRL: Everyone around us – they've all got tellys . . .

SECOND GIRL: Yep.

FIRST GIRL: Isn't that Cliff, or someone, singing?

SECOND GIRL: It sounds like it's Cliff . . . or someone . . . Yep.

FIRST GIRL: It's sort of sad.

SECOND GIRL: Yep.—I like that. [*Pause*] You want to go in the café and listen to the juke-box?

FIRST GIRL: In a minute. When we've looked in the window here. [*Pause.*] It's sort of, maybe, *too* sad – that one.

SECOND GIRL: I like the sad ones. I don't like them cheery ones much.

FIRST GIRL: Maybe it *ain't* Cliff singing.

SECOND GIRL: It *sounds* like him – or someone . . .

[*Pause. The music begins to fade*]

Them toffee-apples look real good. You can see the apple-skin right through the toffee too . . .

FIRST GIRL: Yep. There ain't much toffee . . .

SECOND GIRL: There's plenty toffee. It's just you can see right through it, to the apple-skin.

FIRST GIRL: It'll be mostly water and sugar.

SECOND GIRL: And d'you see them liquorice-straps?

FIRST GIRL: Which?

SECOND GIRL: There – by the sweetie-cigarettes. You see them?

FIRST GIRL: Yep. We ate them too.

SECOND GIRL: So did we.

FIRST GIRL: All of us ate them liquorice-straps.

SECOND GIRL: You know what I always think of when I see them old-fashioned rolled-up liquorice-straps?

FIRST GIRL: No.

SECOND GIRL: Seaweed.

FIRST GIRL: What?

SECOND GIRL: Seaweed. [*Pause*] You ever walked through seaweed – that seaweed that grows by the sea – you know? That seaweed that's all slippery . . . And mostly brown – like them straps of liquorice?

FIRST GIRL: No.

SECOND GIRL: You never walked through it?

FIRST GIRL: No.

SECOND GIRL: You never took your shoes and stockings off – and sort of – paddled through it?

FIRST GIRL: No. I'd be scared to.

SECOND GIRL: Why'd you be scared to?

FIRST GIRL: There might be *things* in it.

SECOND GIRL: What kind of things would there be in seaweed?

FIRST GIRL: Oh, I dunno. Crabs maybe.—Maybe there'd be crabs in it would come and bite you – and – [*Pause*] I'd be *scared* to walk through seaweed.

SECOND GIRL: You just don't know *what's* in seaweed.

FIRST GIRL: That's what I'm telling you. I'd be scared to walk in seaweed.—Maybe there'd even be a lobster in seaweed.—Did you ever go in a rest-ur-ant and *eat* a lobster?

SECOND GIRL: Not yet. But I'm going to – soon.

FIRST GIRL: Maybe – maybe if you go around the place walking in seaweed – maybe you'll never get to eat a lobster. Maybe a lobster will have eaten *you*.

SECOND GIRL: Oh, but it's lovely to walk in seaweed. . . . You take off your shoes and your socks – and you carry them . . . and you go walking all through it – right up to your ankles in it – like you was on a tight-rope . . .

FIRST GIRL: Like you was on what?

SECOND GIRL: Like on a tight-rope – You know, a tight-rope . . .

FIRST GIRL: Oh, a tight-rope, like in the circus?

SECOND GIRL: Yep.

FIRST GIRL: I seen a circus – a real big one – on the telly once . . .

SECOND GIRL: Well, if you saw the circus you'd see a tight-rope.

FIRST GIRL: Yep. There was lions – and things – and some of them elephants too.

SECOND GIRL: Yep? And a lady on a tight-rope?

FIRST GIRL: Yep.

SECOND GIRL: Well, that's a tight-rope.—And walking through seaweed – it's like on a tight-rope – all slippery – and you got to walk carefully. . . . Some of it looks like them straps of liquorice. And there's some, when you walk on it, goes off pop! [*Pause*] That kind's like a lot of little . . . like . . . Well, I dunno, but it can go off pop.

FIRST GIRL: I seen that sort. You can make it pop.

SECOND GIRL: Yep.—You can pop it if you stand on it hard enough.

FIRST GIRL: I popped it myself sometimes.—You know, with my shoes on.

SECOND GIRL: Well, some of the seaweed – it's that funny pop-stuff, and others is kind of longer, like them straps of liquorice there. That's the kind that's always the slipperiest.—You got to walk on it very carefully. . . . You got to walk carefully or maybe you'd slip . . . and then you'd get your dress all wet. . . . So you hold your arms out.

FIRST GIRL: How?

SECOND GIRL: Well, like the lady did on the tight-rope. Holding your arms out – that helps you balance – but you got to take just small steps . . . or you'd maybe fall.

FIRST GIRL: I never went in for walking through seaweed. —Well, I *have* walked through it. But just with my shoes on.

SECOND GIRL: That ain't *really* walking through seaweed.

FIRST GIRL: I'll tell you something, it can spoil your shoes.

SECOND GIRL: I always take my shoes *off*.

FIRST GIRL: So far as I'm concerned, you can keep that seaweed.

SECOND GIRL: Maybe you *have* to walk through seaweed – if you want to get *past* the seaweed and down to the *sea*.

FIRST GIRL: There's a lot of it grows on the top of rocks.

SECOND GIRL: There's a lot of it grows all over the seaside.—And if you want to get to where the sea is, well, you've got to walk through it. . . . But you've got to walk careful . . .

FIRST GIRL: Yep. It can ruin a pair of shoes.

SECOND GIRL: Not if you take them off and carry them.

FIRST GIRL: That's OK for *you* – you ain't *scared* of seaweed.

SECOND GIRL: What's to be scared of in seaweed?

FIRST GIRL: Well, maybe – crabs – or . . .

SECOND GIRL: Or what?

FIRST GIRL: I dunno. You can't *see*, though . . .

SECOND GIRL: Yep. You can't see *what's* in seaweed. I like that. It's sort of exciting . . .

FIRST GIRL: You got funny ideas of what's exciting . . .

SECOND GIRL: You scared of crabs?

FIRST GIRL: Uh-huh. I ain't as scared of crabs as I am of spiders. But I'm scared of crabs. Crabs can *bite*.

SECOND GIRL: I never yet got bit by a crab.

FIRST GIRL: You just wait.—Walking through seaweed.

SECOND GIRL: I walk through it – up to my ankles – in my bare feet – just like a dancer!

FIRST GIRL: You *said* like a telly-tight-rope-lady.

SECOND GIRL: OK like a telly-tight-rope-lady. Or like a dancer. . . . It makes me *feel* like a dancer . . .

FIRST GIRL: I like dancing.

SECOND GIRL: So do I.

FIRST GIRL: I like rock-'n'-roll and jiving.

SECOND GIRL: I like that too – it's lovely.

FIRST GIRL: Everyone goes jiving.

SECOND GIRL: Yep. [*Pause*] You got a boy friend?

FIRST GIRL: Yep. I got lots of them.

SECOND GIRL: You got lots of boy friends?

FIRST GIRL: Yep.

SECOND GIRL: What d'you do with them?

FIRST GIRL: Not much. . . . Go jiving.

SECOND GIRL: That all?

FIRST GIRL: Go to the pictures.

SECOND GIRL: That all?

FIRST GIRL: What else?—Go jiving, go to the pictures. Play the juke-box in a café. What else?

SECOND GIRL: I got a boy friend.

FIRST GIRL: Have you?

SECOND GIRL: Yep. I got a boy friend. And he's sort of special. I mean – I mean I've just the one special boy friend – and do you know what he and I do?

FIRST GIRL: No.

SECOND GIRL: Well, guess – go on. Remember about – about the seaweed, and—. Remember he's my one special boy friend. . . . Now you try and guess what he and I do . . .

FIRST GIRL: Go to the pictures?

SECOND GIRL: No.

FIRST GIRL: Go jiving?

SECOND GIRL: No.

FIRST GIRL: If you had enough money, you could go jiving – or something – every night.

SECOND GIRL: Oh, he and I got plenty money. He and I are *loaded.*— But we don't go jiving.

FIRST GIRL: No? Can't he jive then?

SECOND GIRL: Yep. But he doesn't want to.—He ain't like an ordinary boy. He's special.

FIRST GIRL: All the boys nowadays go jiving.

SECOND GIRL: You're supposed to be guessing what he and I do . . .

FIRST GIRL: No pictures. . . . No jiving. . . . I suppose you go in a café and play the juke-box . . .

SECOND GIRL: No. We never play a juke-box.

FIRST GIRL: Sounds like your boy must be a square.

SECOND GIRL: No, he ain't a square.

FIRST GIRL: Well, what d'you do? You'll have to tell me.

SECOND GIRL: Me and my boy friend – I told you he's special – *we go walking through seaweed.*

FIRST GIRL: You don't!

SECOND GIRL: But we do.—We go – in his car – down to where the sea is, and then – then we take off our shoes . . . and we walk through the seaweed . . . it's ever so lovely!

FIRST GIRL: You must be crackers – you and your boy friend.

SECOND GIRL: We are not crackers. He's a very nice boy. [*Pause*] And while we're walking along through the seaweed – he's ever such a nice boy – he takes hold of my hand . . .

FIRST GIRL: What does he do?

SECOND GIRL: When we're walking?

FIRST GIRL: No, what does he *do*? What does he work at?

SECOND GIRL: He's – he's in advertising.

FIRST GIRL: What's his name?

SECOND GIRL: His first name's Paul.

FIRST GIRL: You ain't just making all of this up, are you?

SECOND GIRL: How'd I be making it up? I told you his name, didn't I – Paul. His name is Paul and he's ever so handsome. . . . He has nice dark hair and he's . . . kind of smooth . . .

FIRST GIRL: It doesn't sound to me like a nice, smooth, handsome boy that's in advertising – a kind of a boy like this Paul – would want to go walking through a lot of seaweed . . .

SECOND GIRL: I beg your pardon, but he *does*. Let me tell you – he wouldn't *mind* getting bit by a crab. [*Pause*] The fact is, he's *fond* of crabs.

FIRST GIRL: Is he?

SECOND GIRL: And we never do get bit.

FIRST GIRL: What kind of a seaweed is that seaweed?

SECOND GIRL: Well, I'll tell you . . . We walk through every kind of seaweed – the liquorice stuff like all them straps there – and also the other poppy kind. . . . And as we walk, we hold hands.

FIRST GIRL: It sounds square to me.

SECOND GIRL: Well, it isn't.—We could take you along with us one day. . . . You could come along with me and Paul, and we could all three of us go walking in the seaweed . . .

FIRST GIRL: I think your Paul must be bats.

SECOND GIRL: He is *not* bats. He's a very sensible boy. He only sometimes gets fed-up of being in – the office. . . . He gets tired of – the office – and on Saturdays – he wants a change. . . . He gets sick-fed-up-to-the-teeth with that old office. . . . So we go and walk through seaweed . . .

FIRST GIRL: Where d'you work yourself?

SECOND GIRL: In a factory.

FIRST GIRL: How come you happened to meet this Paul fellow who's so handsome and works in advertising?

SECOND GIRL: You sound like you don't believe me.

FIRST GIRL: I'm only asking – how come you met him?

SECOND GIRL: We met . . . at a dance. [*Pause*] You know – like me and you did. [*Pause*] I suppose you weren't seeing your boy friends that night?

FIRST GIRL: No.

SECOND GIRL: Sometimes . . . you feel like being more on your own . . . Yep . . .

FIRST GIRL: I never met any handsome smooth fellows – out of advertising – at a dance . . .

SECOND GIRL: Well, maybe you will . . .

FIRST GIRL: I never even *saw* any fellows who looked like that . . .

SECOND GIRL: Well, it's just your luck.—And then Paul and I have the same tastes . . .

FIRST GIRL: Yep. You both like walking through that seaweed . . .

SECOND GIRL: Yep. That's our favourite thing. [*Pause*] Don't you ever get fed-up with going to the pictures? Don't you ever get sick-fed-up-to-the-teeth with just ordinary boys? And work? And all that . . .?

FIRST GIRL: I dunno. I don't think about it.

SECOND GIRL: Where d'you work?

FIRST GIRL: In a factory.

SECOND GIRL: Same as me.

FIRST GIRL: Yep. Same as you. But I never met – at a dance – any handsome fellow out of advertising. I *read* of them in magazines.

I read of *lots* of them in that magazine my Mum gets. . . . Tall, dark and smooth. . . . And come to think of it, *their* name was Paul.

SECOND GIRL: Paul is a very common name in advertising.

FIRST GIRL: Yep. But I never met one *real* such fellow . . .

SECOND GIRL: Maybe you will, though . . . someday.

FIRST GIRL: Maybe. Yep. [*Pause*] I only hope if I do he don't have a taste for walking through seaweed. . . . Seaweed – and eating toffee-apples—

SECOND GIRL: You have to walk through seaweed sometimes – if you want to get down to where the sea is . . .

FIRST GIRL: Who wants to get to the sea?

SECOND GIRL: I do sometimes. I like it. [*Pause*] It ain't like a factory – the sea. It's big – and it's deep, and—. Well, I dunno. But I like the sea.

FIRST GIRL: You're a queer one, you are.

SECOND GIRL: What's the name of *your* boy friend?

FIRST GIRL: I already told you – I ain't got just *one* boy friend. I got lots of boy friends. I got hundreds.

SECOND GIRL: Who?

FIRST GIRL: I can't remember their names off-hand . . .

SECOND GIRL: Are they Beats?

FIRST GIRL: No they ain't.

SECOND GIRL: Do you think I'm a Beat – a Beat girl?

FIRST GIRL: Yep. The things you say – you must be a Beat. Though – well, you ain't *dressed* like a Beat. But walking in seaweed – *that's* sort of a Beat thing . . .

SECOND GIRL: My Paul walks through seaweed. And he ain't a Beat – he's an advertising man.

FIRST GIRL: What do they do in them places?

SECOND GIRL: Advertising places?

FIRST GIRL: Yep. Advertising places. What do they do there?

SECOND GIRL: Well, I dunno. . . . I suppose. . . . Well, they sort of – advertise things . . .

FIRST GIRL: What does *he* do?

SECOND GIRL: Paul?

FIRST GIRL: Yep. What does Paul do in that advertising place?

SECOND GIRL: He.—Well, he never talks much about it. You don't think of – of work when you're walking in the seaweed, see? You feel *romantic*.

FIRST GIRL: All the same you must know what he *does*.

SECOND GIRL: Well, as a matter of fact I do know. What he does is – is – is go to conferences.

FIRST GIRL: Conferences?

SECOND GIRL: Yep.

FIRST GIRL: I read about them conferences in my Mum's magazine . . .

SECOND GIRL: Uh-huh.

FIRST GIRL: It seems like advertising's *all* conferences. There's this boy – the one called Paul, you know – the one who's sort of smooth, and dark, and handsome – and what he does is, go to conferences.

SECOND GIRL: Uh-huh. Well, that's like Paul. Paul goes to conferences.

FIRST GIRL: Then, after the conferences – when they've knocked off advertising – then this boy Paul – this handsome smoothy – he goes and meets his girl and they go to a rest-ur-ant. They sit and eat lobsters and maybe he's *too* smooth.

SECOND GIRL: My Paul isn't too smooth.

FIRST GIRL: Maybe. But what about the other one?

SECOND GIRL: I ain't *got* another one.

FIRST GIRL: Oh ain't you? Come off it . . .

SECOND GIRL: But I *told* you – we're special.

FIRST GIRL: What about the one with ginger hair and a snub nose. The engineer.

SECOND GIRL: I don't *know* any engineers.

FIRST GIRL: I bet *he* wouldn't walk through seaweed though. I bet the ginger one with the snub nose spends *his* Saturdays at a football match.

SECOND GIRL: I don't love *him*. I love Paul.

FIRST GIRL: You don't care about the engineer, eh?

SECOND GIRL: No. If you want to know, I can't stand him.—All he *ever* wants to do is – go and jive.

FIRST GIRL: That's what I said. He does the same things like everyone else does.

SECOND GIRL: But Paul – he's different.

FIRST GIRL: Yep. He's different. You're telling me he is! Any boy who spends his Saturdays just walking through seaweed is different. He's a head-case. [*Pause*] Ain't you even *scared* of what might be in it? Ain't you scared of all them crabs and things?

SECOND GIRL: No. I'm more scared of every day.

FIRST GIRL: What?

SECOND GIRL: Every day. The factory, and all that.—Just working and—. [*Pause*] You know, when we've walked all through the seaweed – that kind like liquorice and the other poppy kind – when we've walked all the way through the seaweed, hand in hand—.

FIRST GIRL: I thought *you* said you walked with your arms held up.

SECOND GIRL: That's right. Like a tight-rope-lady.

FIRST GIRL: Then how come you can hold hands?

SECOND GIRL: Oh, when Paul and I are walking through the seaweed – we only hold up our *outside* hands.

FIRST GIRL: Then how d'you carry your shoes and socks?

SECOND GIRL: What?

FIRST GIRL: If the two of you's holding hands and you're holding up your hands like the telly-tight-rope-lady – you only got *two* hands – how d'you carry your shoes and socks? Eh?

SECOND GIRL: Well – well, what d'you think? We left them up where the car is. See?

FIRST GIRL: Oh? [*Pause*] One of these days you and Paul – you're going to be *sorry* for walking through seaweed.

SECOND GIRL: Why?

FIRST GIRL: You're going to get bit. That's why.

SECOND GIRL: We never get bit. But we just *might* though. That's what's nice about walking through seaweed – that you might get bit . . . just a *little*. . . . [*Pause*] Them crabs don't scare *me*. I ain't scared of crabs. They're kind of on *our* side.

FIRST GIRL: What? Whose side?

SECOND GIRL: Me and Paul's side.

FIRST GIRL: No one's on your side. Except you.

SECOND GIRL: Yes they are. The crabs are. All wee things like crabs and – and wee things like that – they *like* me and Paul. [*Pause*] Do you tell all of them boy friends things?

FIRST GIRL: No. They're just boy friends.

SECOND GIRL: I always tell my Paul *lots* of things.

FIRST GIRL: Do you?

SECOND GIRL: Yep. He's special. I tell him everything.

FIRST GIRL: I can picture it.

SECOND GIRL: What?

FIRST GIRL: You and him – walking in seaweed.—The pair of you standing, walking – right up over the ankles too – in all that seaweed.—All of them crabs ready to bite you – and you and him just standing there telling things . . .

SECOND GIRL: Well, I always feel like telling things there in the seaweed. [*Pause*] And then – like I was saying to you – when we've walked right through it – all through the seaweed – and us holding hands too – holding our hands and telling our secret things—.

FIRST GIRL: What sort of secret things?

SECOND GIRL: Like you tell yourself in bed at night . . .

FIRST GIRL: When I'm in bed at night I go to sleep. If we had the telly I'd sit up later though. Everyone round us has the telly. Only *we* ain't. You feel right out of it.

SECOND GIRL: You can come round some night and see our telly.

FIRST GIRL: That ain't the same as if it was your *own* telly.

SECOND GIRL: No. . . . Well, I was saying – when we've walked all through the seaweed . . .

FIRST GIRL: Yep?

SECOND GIRL: Then me and Paul – he's a real smooth fellow – we come to where the sea is . . .

FIRST GIRL: Yep?

SECOND GIRL: Ain't you listening? We come to the sea.

FIRST GIRL: I'm listening. [*Pause*] I like those records too. . . . All we got at home's an old wireless. . . . My other sister – she's got a radiogram.

SECOND GIRL: We come to the sea and – it's ever so beautiful.

FIRST GIRL: Some of them's beautiful. I like the cheery ones.

SECOND GIRL: I ain't talking about those records on the old juke-box – I'm telling you about Paul and me: we come to *the sea*.

FIRST GIRL: Well, the sea ain't *much* – in my opinion. I don't care *that* much about the sea that I'd risk my life – and spoil my shoes maybe – just walking through a lot of seaweed, all full of crabs and things, to get to it. [*Pause*] You could get bit like that. It just ain't nice.

SECOND GIRL: What ain't nice?

FIRST GIRL: Ain't I telling you? – Seaweed ain't nice. And the sea ain't nice. And having no telly ain't. Eating toffee-apples ain't nice either. I wouldn't put a *toe* in that seaweed . . .

SECOND GIRL: But it's – beautiful – the sea.

FIRST GIRL: Yep. I seen it.

SECOND GIRL: Did you ever dream of it?

FIRST GIRL: I don't have dreams.—Only once I dreamed we'd a telly . . .

SECOND GIRL: Yep.

FIRST GIRL: A great big telly with a screen as big as the screen in a picture-house. Not one of them wee old-fashioned picture-houses screens. . . . A big screen, about a hundred yards across . . .

SECOND GIRL: Yep?

FIRST GIRL: With a plastic-plated cabinet.

SECOND GIRL: I ain't never dreamed of a telly set . . .

FIRST GIRL: Another time I had a dream of a radiogram – and once I dreamed I was married to a disc-jockey.

SECOND GIRL: Well, there you are. You *do* have dreams.

FIRST GIRL: Yep. Well. . . . Maybe . . .

SECOND GIRL: I dreamed – I dreamed of the sea once. . . . It was all – kind of dark – and – it was all big and dark – and—. Well, it was – beautiful!

FIRST GIRL: It was a beautiful radiogram in my dream. It was kind of Hi-Fi Stereoscopic. Posh! You didn't even have to press the button. You just had to *think* and it went and switched itself on.

SECOND GIRL: Yep? You know what the sea was like in my dream?

FIRST GIRL: It was Hi-Fi Stereoscopic – with *five* extra loudspeakers.

SECOND GIRL: It was just kind of like *home* – it was just kind of like what a *real home* is . . .

FIRST GIRL: What?

SECOND GIRL: I said – the sea in my dream – it was all big and dark and – just like home!

FIRST GIRL: You talk like a funny picture I saw.

SECOND GIRL: I could have stayed there by it – forever!

FIRST GIRL: It made me want to giggle. *Everyone* giggled.

SECOND GIRL: But my Mum came and waked me up.

FIRST GIRL: What?

SECOND GIRL: I had to wake up – out of my dream.

FIRST GIRL: I wonder why I dreamed of a great big radiogram?

SECOND GIRL: I suppose you'd like to *have* a great big radiogram.

FIRST GIRL: Yep.

SECOND GIRL: Maybe you could come with us down to the sea. Or – well, if Paul had to work some Saturday – if he got asked to do overtime – at advertising – we could go there . . . just the two of us.

FIRST GIRL: And walk through that seaweed—!?

SECOND GIRL: I could hold your hand – like Paul holds my hand –.

FIRST GIRL: You ain't like a magazine fellow that would make me feel all right about that seaweed . . .

SECOND GIRL: I'd hold it tight.—Ever so tight. [*Pause*] You and I – we could hold hands – we could go walking – like dancers – like on a tight-rope – all down through all that seaweed – and we'd tell each other things – all our secret things.—Yep, you and me – we could walk through the seaweed – all the way – right to the sea! [*Pause*] You got to walk through seaweed or – or you don't get anywhere. And seaweed – it's full of crabs and things. . . . But you got to walk through it – hand in hand – with some other person – because it's lovely too – you got to walk – like a dancer – like two dancers – all through the seaweed – right to the sea . . .!

FIRST GIRL: All my life I kept out of seaweed. I stayed away from seaweed. It ain't well – nice stuff. You can go and walk in all that seaweed – you can go if you want to – but not with *me*!

SECOND GIRL: I like the look of them toffee-apples . . .

FIRST GIRL: They're just for kids. [*Pause*] Let's go in the café now. [*Pause*] I like that one that's on the juke-box. Though it's kind of sad. . . . Come on, let's go . . .

SECOND GIRL: Yep. Let's go in the café and play the juke-box.— Maybe some of all of them boy friends of yours will be in the café – perhaps.

[*The music grows louder. It is a record – something like – Bobby Darin's* 'Beyond The Sea']

Somewhere . . .
Beyond the sea . . .

[*The two girls saunter off as the music grows still louder – then slowly fades*]

THE WILD DOGS IN WINTER

CHARACTERS

PUBLICAN

FIRST DOMINO PLAYER

SECOND DOMINO PLAYER

THIRD DOMINO PLAYER

THE SMITH

THE WOODSMAN

MACLEISH

SCENE: *The bar of an hotel in a Scotch village. It is a very cold, frosty, winter night. Through the window we can see the suggestion of a street with lamps, ending at pinewoods against a frosty sky. A full moon is just rising through the pines.*

Behind the bar stands the PUBLICAN, *a pleasant but simple young man, he wears a sports jacket. There are also five customers in the bar, as follows:–*

At the top of the bar three DOMINO PLAYERS.

Alone, and halfway down the bar, the SMITH.

In front of the pine-log fire, the WOODSMAN.

All five are in their working clothes. These are black and resemble mourning clothes. Between them, and now full of a thin, white cold haze, the empty spaces of the bar stand defined.

As the CURTAIN *rises there is a silence, dreary and menacing, like that in a wood at dusk. The* PUBLICAN *is reading a newspaper. The clicking of the dominoes as they are set down on the bar-counter suggests frozen wood-chips flying from an axe.*

In the distance, a dog howls mournfully.

Then:

FIRST DOMINO PLAYER: Listen to *him* . . .

SECOND DOMINO PLAYER: Aye, just listen to him – shut up! . . . Double-six, is it? . . . Pass.

THIRD DOMINO PLAYER: You're passing . . . Right. Double-six . . .— *Shut-up.*

SECOND DOMINO PLAYER: Aye. *I'd* shut you up, you brute . . .

[*The dog stops howling, a silence. Then the* PUBLICAN *coughs, gives a twitch to his newspaper, looks at each customer in turn, and says sociably*]:

PUBLICAN: I see they got those two dogs . . .

SMITH [*tight-lipped*]: Aye . . .

WOODSMAN [*grimly*]: Aye . . .

FIRST DOMINO PLAYER: Me again, is it? . . . Aye, they got those dogs, so I heard.

PUBLICAN: Yes, but it's here, in my newspaper . . . There's a whole paragraph about it, on the middle page . . .

FIRST DOMINO PLAYER [*looks up*]: Is there? A whole paragraph about the two wild dogs?

PUBLICAN [*nods*]: Yes, there is . . .

FIRST DOMINO PLAYER: Well, fancy that! Can you beat that—! And is there a picture as well?

PUBLICAN: No . . . No, there's no picture . . .

WOODSMAN [*with hostility, as if it were an accusation*]: There aren't *any* pictures in that paper of his!—No pictures and no football . . . Call that a newspaper—? [*Glares at the* PUBLICAN. *turns and spits. the spit sizzles in the hot, red flames*]

PUBLICAN [*mildly*]: Football – yes, there is, Woodsman.

WOODSMAN: Where? Where's the football? – Just show me where the football is . . .

PUBLICAN [*turns over the page. Holds the paper up. Points*]: Here it is . . . Here's the football here . . .

WOODSMAN [*laughs harshly*]: What! That one wee paragraph? Call *that* football . . .!? There's nothing in that paper but a lot of politics and . . . and tripe! I wonder you don't stop it and get yourself a proper paper, so I do!

PUBLICAN: Tripe . . .?

WOODSMAN: Aye, that's what I said. No pictures . . . A lot of tripe.

PUBLICAN: Well, Woodsman, you're a customer and I don't want to argue with you, but I can tell that this newspaper is – well, reliable. It prints, well, the news . . . It just prints the news and you can rely on it . . . You read it and you know it's true, and . . . and not just sensational. It's a decent newspaper, don't you think so, Smith?

[*He looks at the* SMITH *for support. there is a silence. a harsh shuffling of dominoes. then*]

SMITH: I'm not saying anything. It's none of my business. You and the Woodsman can fight it out . . .

PUBLICAN [*taken aback*]: Fight it out . . .? But . . . Oh, here now . . . I was just being sociable. I wasn't arguing. But I think a pub ought to be – well, a friendly place – a sort of – of social club—.

SECOND DOMINO PLAYER [*looks up. Cuts in*]: Well, there *is* a club in the village already.

THIRD DOMINO PLAYER: Aye, that's right. There *is* a club. There's the Institute, across the bridge . . . Double-six you want, is it? . . . Hmm . . .

PUBLICAN: Well, yes, there's the Institute . . . I know that. But it's only for men – for ex-service men. And . . . And well, take the Woodsman there—. Why doesn't the Woodsman bring his Missus in for a drink one night?

WOODSMAN: Eh? Bring the Missus to the pub? Not me—!

PUBLICAN: Why *not*? I think you ought to . . .

SECOND DOMINO PLAYER: Aye, *you* think he ought to . . . *You* want her to sit there drinking a lot of gins all night. [*Points to an empty chair that stands by the hearth*]

THIRD DOMINO PLAYER: Aye, *he* wants the profit! – A lot of bloomin gins at five bob a glass—!

PUBLICAN: No, I don't . . . I mean, well, I don't mean I *don't* want to make a profit, but . . . But I've told you before – I've told you all before that in my opinion a pub ought to be a place for a quiet pint. A quiet pint and a friendly chat . . .

SECOND DOMINO PLAYER [*laughs*]: A quiet pint!—It's quiet enough in here tonight, all right . . .!

FIRST DOMINO PLAYER: Well, what do you expect, seeing it's Thursday? Night before pay-night . . .

THIRD DOMINO PLAYER: Aye, it'll be busy enough in here tomorrow night . . .

SECOND DOMINO PLAYER:—And we'll be seeing the Woodsman in with his Missus—! [*Laughs*]

WOODSMAN: Aye, you will . . . And I *don't* think—! [*Turns and spits*].

THIRD DOMINO PLAYER: Aye, a pub's no place for The Women . . .

PUBLICAN: Well, I don't want to argue but I think it *is*. [*Pause*] You know what I'm going to do with this pub? I'm going to take away all that black woodwork—[*Points*] and I'm going to have it painted a nice, bright colour, . . . Cream. And then, over there, where that empty chair is – over there by the fireplace – I'm going to put a little, low table . . . And then another opposite it, too . . . with a *cloth* . . .

THIRD DOMINO PLAYER: For the Woodsman's Missus *that* will be—! [*Laughs*]

PUBLICAN: Well, yes, for the Woodsman's Missus . . . For anyone's Missus – I'm going to change all this . . . I'm going to make *my* pub into a nice, bright, friendly place – like the pubs you see down South . . .

SECOND DOMINO PLAYER: This isn't down South . . .

THIRD DOMINO PLAYER: No, this isn't . . . 'A quiet pint!'—Here, give us a whisky here, will you?

PUBLICAN [*turns to pour it*]: A whisky . . .

WOODSMAN: And while you're about it this fire could be doing with another log.

PUBLICAN: Well, just take a log, Woodsman. Isn't there a whole box of logs? That's what I put the logs there for – for any customer to help himself.

WOODSMAN [*throws a log on the fire*]: To help himself . . . Thank you. We're a bit short of logs, this weather. The Missus could just be doing with a few of these logs here . . . [*Laughs harshly*]

FIRST DOMINO PLAYER: That isn't what he means . . . And *you* shouldn't be short of logs anyway . . .

PUBLICAN [*passes it across the counter*]: A whisky . . .

THIRD DOMINO PLAYER: I hope that's good measure . . . Right you are . . . Keep the change.

PUBLICAN: Keep . . . Come on, another threepence . . . [*Takes it*] Thank you. [*Puts the money in the till*]

WOODSMAN [*rubs his hands*]: Brr! It's cold in here. Bloomin' freezing! You could do with *two* fires in your posh new pub . . .

SECOND DOMINO PLAYER: Aye, you could, too. It's like out-of-doors in here tonight . . .

THIRD DOMINO PLAYER: Aye, it's like out-of-doors . . . And look at that – look – there's a bloomin' mist like you'd see in a wood . . . See?

FIRST DOMINO PLAYER: That's the cold makes that mist . . . There's a hard frost.

PUBLICAN [*makes a joke but it doesn't go down*]: Yes, and if there's a mist like you'd see in a wood, I must say that my customers – you're so chatty – you'd make good trees—! [*Laughs pleasantly*]

WOODSMAN [*with blank hostility*]: What do you mean?

SECOND DOMINO PLAYER: Aye, what do you mean – we'd make good trees?

PUBLICAN [*abashed*]: It was only a joke . . . It's the way you stand there, and . . . your black clothes . . .

WOODSMAN: What's wrong with our clothes?

PUBLICAN: Nothing . . . There's nothing wrong with them . . . It was just a silly joke . . .

WOODSMAN: Oh. It was just a joke . . . Well, I can't see that it was funny, saying we was like trees. What do *you* know about trees?

PUBLICAN: I don't know anything about trees . . .

WOODSMAN: Well, there you are . . .

FIRST DOMINO PLAYER: Maybe it *wouldn't* be so cold in here if the Woodsman was to stand away from that fire.

PUBLICAN [*to the* WOODSMAN, *politely*]: Your clothes are scorching, do you know?

WOODSMAN [*not budging*]: What?

PUBLICAN: Your clothes are scorching. Look at the smoke . . . See . . .

THIRD DOMINO PLAYER: Smoke? That isn't smoke . . .

WOODSMAN: No, it isn't smoke that. It's steam . . . My pockets – see? – are all full of pine-bark. It must have been frozen and now it's thawing. Your pockets get that way – full of bark – from working in the wood.

THIRD DOMINO PLAYER: Aye, so they do . . . How many trees did you take down this day, Woodsman?

WOODSMAN [*shrugs*]: Can't say . . . But I took down plenty. Take a look out that window . . . Look against the sky there . . . See the gaps?

THIRD DOMINO PLAYER [*looks through the window*]: Aye. There's a lot of gaps . . .

FIRST DOMINO PLAYER: Looks like a saw-blade with a lot of teeth missing . . .

THIRD DOMINO PLAYER: So it does, too. It's them sharp pines . . .

WOODSMAN: I'm the man to take them down, sir . . . Look at that axe . . . [*Lifts it up. It has been leaning against the mantelpiece*] Feel that blade . . .

PUBLICAN: Sharp . . .?

THIRD DOMINO PLAYER: Aye. Like a razor . . .

FIRST DOMINO PLAYER [*is still looking through the window*]: And see that moon . . . Full moon . . . *It's* sharp . . .

SECOND DOMINO PLAYER: Aye, it's full . . . and there's hard frost . . .

FIRST DOMINO PLAYER: Aye, just look at the frost there . . . under the lamps . . . See?

PUBLICAN [*goes to the top of the bar to look out the window*]: Well, just look at that now . . . You can see it . . . You can actually see it sparkling there under the lamps.

FIRST DOMINO PLAYER: Aye . . . Like a lot of wee *chimes* . . . only you can *see* them . . . Sort of wee, silver chimes – thousands and thousands . . . And don't those pinewoods just look *black*—?

SECOND DOMINO PLAYER: You're a bloomin' poet, you are! What'd you expect them to be? Yellow! . . . Come on, it's you to play . . .

FIRST DOMINO PLAYER: Me to play? No, it isn't . . . I put down that three, there. It's *you.*

SECOND DOMINO PLAYER: Oh, you did, eh – did you? [*The dog howls again*] – Listen to him! – Shut up! – Shut up!

THIRD DOMINO PLAYER: Aye, it's the moon does it . . . *Shut-up!* [*The dog stops howling*]

FIRST DOMINO PLAYER: What does the paper say about those two dogs?

PUBLICAN [*not listening*]: Er . . . what?

FIRST DOMINO PLAYER: Your newspaper . . . What does it say about the two wild dogs?

WOODSMAN: That bloomin' paper—! [*Turns and spits*]

PUBLICAN [*delighted*]: Oh . . . Oh, my paper . . . Well, there's a whole paragraph, all about it, on the middle page . . .

FIRST DOMINO PLAYER: Fancy—! A big newspaper like that . . . and there's a whole paragraph about those dogs here . . .

SECOND DOMINO PLAYER: What do you mean, fancy?—That was a *sensation*, that was . . .

PUBLICAN [*has turned back to the middle page*]: Here it is, here . . . I – I'll read it to you, shall I? Shall I read it? [*Looks at the customers*]

FIRST DOMINO PLAYER: Aye, read it . . .

SECOND DOMINO PLAYER: Aye, go on. We might as well hear what it says about those dogs here . . .

WOODSMAN: A lot of tripe—! [*He disassociates himself. Looks out the window. The others prepare to listen*]

PUBLICAN [*reads, a little nervously, but he unconsciously assumes the manner of a missionary reading to natives*]: 'From our special correspondent –.'

SECOND DOMINO PLAYER [*interrupts*]: From *what*—? What did you say?

PUBLICAN: Our special correspondent.

THIRD DOMINO PLAYER: Who's he?

PUBLICAN: I don't know. I don't know who he is . . . He might be anyone.

SECOND DOMINO PLAYER: Aye. He might be the Smith, there . . . Eh, Smith?

THIRD DOMINO PLAYER: The Smith's very quiet tonight . . .

SMITH [*grins and looks about slyly*]

SECOND DOMINO PLAYER: He's thinking on something . . .

THIRD DOMINO PLAYER: Aye, so I see . . .

PUBLICAN [*reads*]: 'From our special correspondent. Wednesday. It is reported from here that the two dogs responsible for the destruction of fifteen sheep returned yesterday to their owner, a local shepherd, who has personally destroyed both dogs. As was already reported this outbreak of sheep-worrying has been the severest the district has ever known so far. It will be recalled that the two dogs, one of which was a mere puppy, remained at large for a fortnight and, despite the severe and frosty weather which favoured their pursuers, were neither heard nor sighted once. Their destruction by their owner yesterday has ended the tension and brought a general relief . . .' [*Pause*] Well, there you are . . . That's what it says. [*A silence. Then to the* SMITH]: Well, Smith?

SMITH [*looks at the* PUBLICAN *in a blank, puzzled way*]: That's a queer thing . . .

PUBLICAN: What's queer?

SMITH: That.—That what you just read out the newspaper – it's the same as happened *here* . . .

PUBLICAN: What—? But it *is* the same, Smith . . . It's *about* what happened here . . .

SMITH: You mean that *that* – in the newspaper – that's about this place? What happened *here*?

PUBLICAN: But of course it is, Smith. How—. What did you think it was about, eh?

SECOND DOMINO PLAYER [*jeers*]: *He* thought it happened on the moon—! [*Laughs*]

SMITH: Aye. Aye, and so I *did*, too. I thought it must have happened somewhere on the moon . . .

FIRST DOMINO PLAYER [*as the others laugh*]: Well, I can *see* how he thought that . . . It's the way it's written that's got you mixed-up, Smith.

SMITH: Aye, it's a queer way of writing . . .

PUBLICAN: Well, it isn't sensational . . .

FIRST DOMINO PLAYER: Aye, that's right. It's cold . . . Cold and . . . and sort of distant . . . And that's why the Smith thought it couldn't be *here* and must be somewhere *far-away* . . . like up on the moon . . .

SMITH [*as the other two* DOMINO PLAYERS *laugh*]: Well, I don't know what you're laughing for . . . Because the way that paper says it, it makes the bloomin' sheep sound like frozen mutton-carcases. Aye. Aye, it makes them sound like frozen mutton-carcases, the same as you see carried into the butcher's there. And it makes this place here sound as far-away as – as the moon . . . [*Pause*] How do you know it wasn't somewhere far-away?

PUBLICAN: What, Smith – on the moon? But they don't *have* sheep on the moon . . .

THIRD DOMINO PLAYER: I read somewhere as they have canals . . .

PUBLICAN: Well, perhaps they do have canals . . . That's one theory. But everyone knows they don't have sheep.

SMITH: Who says so? *You* don't know . . . You haven't *been* on the moon, have you? And what I say is, if they do have sheep there, then they're like frozen mutton-carcases . . . Aye.

SECOND DOMINO PLAYER: Well, so what if they are like frozen mutton-carcases?

SMITH: Eh?— So what? Well they say those dogs *here* had the sheep torn all into wee, bloody bits . . . [*A pause. He grins slyly*]: I'll have a pint.

PUBLICAN: A pint, Smith . . . Right . . . [*Draws it*]

SMITH [*takes it. Pays*]: Here . . .

PUBLICAN: Thank you. [*Turns his back and puts the money in the till*]

> [*The* SMITH *holds his pint-glass up to the light. He is looking to see if the beer has anything wrong with it. The stage turns red – the red of the electric-light seen through the beer – the red of a frosted winter sun. The* PUBLICAN *turns and sees the* SMITH]

PUBLICAN [*as the light returns to normal*]: Beer all right, Smith?

SMITH: Aye. We'll say it's all right . . . Can't *see* anything wrong with it . . .

WOODSMAN [*turns his head from the window. He is steaming profusely and is livid with rage. He has barely been restraining himself*]: Aye, the beer's maybe all right, but the newspaper – that paper of yours – it's wrong—!

PUBLICAN [*gasps*]: Wrong—?

WOODSMAN: Aye. Wrong. It's wrong about the dogs. It was the shepherd shot the old dog but the young dog – *it* was shot by MacLeish.

PUBLICAN: [*repeats in astonishment*]: The young dog . . . was shot by . . MacLeish . . .

WOODSMAN: Aye, by MacLeish. And your paper – your fancy paper without pictures – says the shepherd shot *both* dogs.

[*A general murmur of agreement.* PUBLICAN *is in a quandary. he can neither disbelieve the* WOODSMAN *nor bring himself to believe that his newspaper can possibly be wrong*]

PUBLICAN [*not knowing what to say*]: But see here, Woodsman . . .

WOODSMAN [*snaps*]: What?

PUBLICAN: It says—. I mean to say—. Well, I mean, this is a reliable newspaper . . .

WOODSMAN: Is it—? I told you already you want to stop it and get yourself a proper paper! Trash! [*Turns and spits*]

PUBLICAN: But—. Well, what I mean is, couldn't you have made a mistake about the two dogs, Woodsman?

WOODSMAN: Me? – *Me* make a mistake? It's your paper that's made the mistake [*Repeats*]. The shepherd shot the old dog – the young dog was shot by MacLeish!

PUBLICAN [*almost to himself*]: By MacLeish—! My paper's wrong—! [*He folds it up and, shaking his head, stuffs it down behind the till. A corner still protrudes like a clean handkerchief from a top-pocket. There has been a silence. The dog howls again, very mournfully.*]

SECOND DOMINO PLAYER: Shut up, you brute!

THIRD DOMINO PLAYER: Aye, – *I'd* shut you up, all right . . . Howling . . .

PUBLICAN [*has turned round. He makes a fresh attempt at some light conversation*]: Those two dogs – the wild dogs – they must have been psychopathic doing a thing like that, eh?

SECOND DOMINO PLAYER: Psycho – what did you say? [*Laughs*]

PUBLICAN: Psycho*pathic*. Psychopathic . . . *you* know— [*Taps his forehead*] A bit off . . . Crackers . . . Bats . . .

THIRD DOMINO PLAYER: How? How bats?

PUBLICAN: How? Well, they killed fifteen good, live sheep, didn't they?

SMITH [*grins slyly*]: Aye. They killed fifteen *live* sheep . . . Had them all torn into wee, bloody bits . . . [*He is grinning to himself and is all excited*]

FIRST DOMINO PLAYER: Did they, though? Who said so?

SECOND DOMINO PLAYER: Aye, they did though. That's right. I was out myself on one of the drives they had . . . We went through the wood there – [*Points through the window*] – right up through the wood and out the hill, too, but we never saw no sign of the dogs.

THIRD DOMINO PLAYER: Well, they laid low and you missed them . . .

SECOND DOMINO PLAYER: Aye, we missed them, all right. But it was queer. There was a whole line of us, see? – a whole long line, and we was all shouting – 'Hi, hi, hi!' [*Imitates the frenzied shouting of beaters*] – and beating on the trees with our sticks, see? And it was still—.

THIRD DOMINO PLAYER: Aye, it was still right enough. Hard frost . . .

SECOND DOMINO PLAYER: Aye. You could have heard a leaf fall, it was that still—.

SMITH [*cuts in*]: Pint.

PUBLICAN: Pint, Smith . . . [*Draws it*]

THIRD DOMINO PLAYER: Another pint? What's up with *you* tonight? You must have drunk that last one double-quick . . .

SMITH [*grins*]: Aye.

FIRST DOMINO PLAYER: I think he likes all this about the dogs.

SECOND DOMINO PLAYER: Aye, the Smith's enjoying himself tonight . . . He's celebrating, the bloodthirsty old—.

PUBLICAN [*cuts in. Passes it*]: – Pint. [*Takes the money. Puts it in the till*]

[*The* SMITH *takes the beer. he holds it to the light again. the stage turns red. the* SECOND DOMINO PLAYER *continues*]:

SECOND DOMINO PLAYER [*while the light is red*]: Aye, we was all shouting and beating the trees – 'Hi, hi, hi' – like a lot of bloomin' madmen . . . And it was that still in the wood . . . still and frosty, see? The ferns was all frosted and stifflike – like the hair on a scared dog's coat––. [*The dog howls. Pause. Then*] But we never saw the dogs – neither of them – never saw a sign of them – though we knew they was *there*.

PUBLICAN [*sociably*]: How did you know they were there?

SECOND DOMINO PLAYER: Well, by the sheep, see?

PUBLICAN: You mean the sheep there were newly killed?

SECOND DOMINO PLAYER: Aye . . . The sheep there was newly killed . . .

SMITH [*grins*]: They was all torn into wee, bloody bits . . . [*Lowers his glass. The light returns to normal*]

SECOND DOMINO PLAYER: Aye, they was a mess all right, the sheep . . .

PUBLICAN: And they killed fifteen altogether?

SECOND DOMINO PLAYER: Well, aye, they did – if you count the ones the farmers had to destroy.

PUBLICAN [*shakes his head*]: Well, all I can say is, they must have been psycho – must have been bats, doing a thing like that.

THIRD DOMINO PLAYER: How?

PUBLICAN: How? Good heavens, man. Just think . . . Just think of *the expense* involved!

THIRD DOMINO PLAYER: Aye, that's right. The expense . . . Fifteen sheep . . .

PUBLICAN: Yes. Fifteen good sheep – those cost a lot of money, you know . . .

SECOND DOMINO PLAYER: Aye, they must have been a *bit* cracked, but – well, they wasn't so stupid when we were having our drive after them, eh?

FIRST DOMINO PLAYER: I don't know that they *were* cracked . . .

PUBLICAN: You don't think they were cracked . . .?

FIRST DOMINO PLAYER: No. Everyone likes to break out *sometime* . . .

PUBLICAN: Break out sometime?

FIRST DOMINO PLAYER: Aye.–– You get fed up. You like to have a good burst-up – go on the spree – just for a change.

SECOND DOMINO PLAYER: Aye, so you do. You like a good burst-up for a bit of a change.

THIRD DOMINO PLAYER: Well, you had *that* all right last week . . .! Had to carry you home, we did!

PUBLICAN: Well, all I can say is that you can't call the senseless destruction of fifteen valuable sheep a 'bit of a burst-up'. I say, let a man have a night out now and then if he wants to . . . But he ought to take his Missus along sometimes, *too* . . .

THIRD DOMINO PLAYER: Take the Missus on a burst-up—!

PUBLICAN: No. Not for a burst-up. For a quiet pint . . .

THIRD DOMINO PLAYER: A *pint* – for the Missus –? [*Laughs*] I can see my Missus drinking a pint—!

PUBLICAN [*confused*]: No, I mean—. Well, I mean to say . . . What I mean to say is, think of the *farmers* – think of the farmers who *owned* the sheep. Suppose these sheep had been *your* property? No . . . [*Shakes his head*] Those two dogs *must* have been *bats*.

FIRST DOMINO PLAYER: Well, that's right enough. I never thought of that. Think of the farmers – *and* of the shepherd. I'll bet *he* was fair upset.

SECOND DOMINO PLAYER: Aye, he *was*, too, so I heard . . .

FIRST DOMINO PLAYER: Fancy – a whole fortnight – and knowing it was *your* dogs was killing all those sheep . . . Eh?

THIRD DOMINO PLAYER: Aye, and sheep-dogs . . . Fancy them as did it being *sheep*-dogs . . . And they say they was *good* dogs, both of them, too . . .

SECOND DOMINO PLAYER: Well, so they were. That old one – it was a grand worker, and so was the pup . . .

PUBLICAN: Just a pup, was it?

SECOND DOMINO PLAYER: Aye. But you'd have thought the old dog would have had more sense.

FIRST DOMINO PLAYER: Aye, you can't blame the young dog . . .

THIRD DOMINO PLAYER: No, you can't. It was led astray, I bet.

SMITH [*grins*]: Aye . . . Out on the spree . . . And when they went home their coats was all matted, and their jaws . . . was dripping with blood . . .

THIRD DOMINO PLAYER: Is that a fact? Dripping with blood . . .

FIRST DOMINO PLAYER: I never heard that . . . Who said so? Anyway, it was the old dog as went home first . . .

WOODSMAN [*joins in*]: Aye, it went home first and the shepherd shot it – but the young dog was shot by MacLeish—!

PUBLICAN [*is embarrassed. Turns and tries to tuck the newspaper right out of sight*]: MacLeish – do I know him?

THIRD DOMINO PLAYER: Well, if you don't know him, you ought to. He's *been* in here . . .

PUBLICAN: Oh, has he?

THIRD DOMINO PLAYER: Aye. Once or twice . . .

PUBLICAN: MacLeish . . .? MacLeish . . .? What does he look like?

FIRST DOMINO PLAYER: A small man . . . Wears a greatcoat . . .

SECOND DOMINO PLAYER: Has a jeep . . . Stays up the glen . . .

THIRD DOMINO PLAYER: Aye, you don't see him often . . . And when you do he won't wait long.—He just drinks a whisky and goes straight out . . .

FIRST DOMINO PLAYER: Aye, he's a quiet chap . . . Doesn't gossip.

THIRD DOMINO PLAYER: Well, who does? Do you think *I* do?

PUBLICAN: Wait a minute . . . I think I know him. Would he be carrying a *book*?

SECOND DOMINO PLAYER: Aye, that's him!

THIRD DOMINO PLAYER: Aye, with a book . . . [*Laughs*] That's him!

PUBLICAN: Now I have him . . . So that's MacLeish . . .

WOODSMAN: Aye, and you want to write and tell your paper – that's MacLeish who shot the young dog!

PUBLICAN: I remember he came in one night and he was carrying a book and he set it down, you see, on the counter – he was standing [*Points*] there, where the Smith is – and it got all wet . . . in a pool of beer.

SECOND DOMINO PLAYER: In a pool of beer – his book did—! [*Laughs*] He might have sued you for that! [*Laughs again*]

PUBLICAN: [*looks at the* WOODSMAN]: So that's MacLeish . . . who shot the young dog . . .

THIRD DOMINO PLAYER: How come, I wonder, *he* shot it?

SECOND DOMINO PLAYER: Must have been over there, at the shepherd's place, when it came home, most likely. Aye . . .

FIRST DOMINO PLAYER: Aye. Maybe he was, too. Maybe he'd been thinking how the shepherd would be all upset, and—.

PUBLICAN: [*cuts in*]: I'll bet he *was* upset, too . . . Would he have to *pay* for all those sheep, do you think?

SECOND DOMINO PLAYER: No. No, he wouldn't. Not so long as he'd gone and reported the dogs was missing he wouldn't have to pay . . .

PUBLICAN: That was lucky . . .

FIRST DOMINO PLAYER: Aye, but still . . . Fancy his having to shoot his own dog . . .

WOODSMAN: The *old* dog—.

FIRST DOMINO PLAYER: Aye, the old dog . . . But having to shoot it – I'll bet he felt terrible . . .

PUBLICAN: Still, it was crackers. You couldn't do anything *but* shoot it, could you?

FIRST DOMINO PLAYER: No. No, I suppose not . . .

SMITH [*grins slyly*]: Their jaws was all dripping . . . with blood . . .

SECOND DOMINO PLAYER: Is that a fact?

SMITH [*holds his glass up. The stage turns red*]: Aye . . . [*Grins*] Aye . . . Dripping with blood . . .

SECOND DOMINO PLAYER [impressed]: Well, that'll be right . . . There was a whole line of us – a whole long line of us – and we was all shouting – 'Hi, hi, hi!' – and beating the trees . . . And it was a big, red sun. Still . . . And a big, red frosted sun . . . And we never seen the dogs, see?— Not a sign of them . . .

[*The dog howls mournfully*]

You'd come to a clearing and you'd *think* you saw one . . . that you saw one – saw one – *there*! [*Points into the corner. They all turn and look as if expecting to see the dog*] – And there was nothing at all . . . nothing at all . . .

[*The dog stops howling. The* SMITH *lowers his glass*]

THIRD DOMINO PLAYER: But you saw the sheep . . .?

SECOND DOMINO PLAYER: Eh? . . . Oh aye . . .

THIRD DOMINO PLAYER: Brr, it's cold in here, eh . . .?

SECOND DOMINO PLAYER: Aye, it's fair freezing . . .

THIRD DOMINO PLAYER: Aye, it is. Fair freezing. And there's a bloomin' mist like you'd see in a wood . . .

SECOND DOMINO PLAYER: Aye . . .

[*The black window has been slowly whitening as a jeep drives down the street. We see its headlights and hear its engine. Then we hear it stop outside the bar door. The door opens. A small man enters. He wears a greatcoat and carries a book below his arm. They all look at him with their mouths open. A lean, grey draught slinks at his heels. Then it sinks away into the corner. There is silence . . .*]

MACLEISH [*crosses to the bar. Stands between the* SMITH *and the* DOMINO

PLAYERS. *then, in a slow, husky voice*]: Good evening. [*No answer*] Good evening . . . a whisky, please.

PUBLICAN [*comes out of the trance they have all been in*]: Eh? Oh . . . Oh yes, a whisky . . . It's—. I mean, you'll be Mr MacLeish . . .? Yes?

MACLEISH: [*surprised*]: Yes . . .?

PUBLICAN: It was you . . . [*Turns. Pours the whisky*] I mean . . . Well, what I mean is, we were just talking about the two wild dogs . . .

MACLEISH: *Wild* – dogs? Thank you. [*Pays. Takes the whisky. Crosses to the empty chair by the hearth. Sits down. Stares dreamily into his glass*]

WOODSMAN: Aye, that's right. We was just talking about the two wild dogs . . . It was the shepherd shot the old one but – sure it was *you* shot the young dog, Mr MacLeish?

MACLEISH [*slowly, softly, looking into his whisky-glass*]: Shot the young dog . . .? Yes, I did . . .

[*A pause. Then*]

SECOND DOMINO PLAYER: You were over there – at the shepherd's place?

MACLEISH [*nods*]: Yes . . . Yes, I was. Just by . . . chance . . .

THIRD DOMINO PLAYER: And saw the old dog, did you?

MACLEISH [*nods slowly*]: Yes, I did . . . I . . . I helped to bury it . . .

SECOND DOMINO PLAYER [*disappointed*]: Oh . . . Oh, you only saw it *after* it was shot . . .

MACLEISH: Eh? Yes, after it was shot . . .

THIRD DOMINO PLAYER: And the young dog – I bet it was savage . . . [SMITH *grins slyly*]

SECOND DOMINO PLAYER: Aye, savage – I bet it was savage!

MACLEISH [*shakes his head slowly*]: Savage . . .? No . . . No, it wasn't . . . No . . . Not a bit . . .

THIRD DOMINO PLAYER [*carried away*]: Aye, it was though . . . It was savage . . . Its coat was all matted and its jaws was . . . dripping with blood . . .

SMITH [*grins*]: Blood . . .

SECOND DOMINO PLAYER: Aye . . . And when you shot it – was it tied on a rope? I bet it was on a rope—.

THIRD DOMINO PLAYER: Aye. On a rope. Snarling . . .

SECOND DOMINO PLAYER: Aye . . . You had it on a rope and – what happened then?

MACLEISH [*slowly*]: On a rope . . .? No . . . No, it wasn't on a rope . . .

THIRD DOMINO PLAYER: It *wasn't* on a rope—?

MACLEISH: No . . . It was in the kitchen, you see . . . just lying in the corner in the kitchen, and . . .

THIRD DOMINO PLAYER: And—?

SECOND DOMINO PLAYER: And—?

SMITH [*grins*]

MACLEISH [*reluctantly, very slowly and softly*]: And, well, I just whistled it round to the shed, you see . . . And . . . and it came along with me – as good as . . . as good as gold . . . Of course, you see, it was a wee bit scared . . . It knew it had done wrong, and . . . And well, you see, it saw I had the gun . . .

SECOND DOMINO PLAYER: It saw you had the gun—!

THIRD DOMINO PLAYER: It saw the gun—!

SMITH [*grins*]: The gun . . .

MACLEISH: Yes . . . Yes, it saw the gun . . . It *knew*, you see . . . And it lay down on the floor . . . on the floor, looking up at me . . . looking up at me and wagging its tail . . . And . . . [*A pause. All at once he raises his whisky-glass. Drains it. Then*]: And well, you see, that was all . . . . . [*Stands up*] Yes, you see, that was all . . . [*Sets his glass on the mantelpiece. Looks around*] Well, good night everyone. Good night.

[*He goes out. They look after him in silence. The jeep starts up. Its sound is loud then fades away. The dog howls briefly and mournfully. Then*]:

WOODSMAN: [*harshly. He is triumphant*]: I told you! – just like I told you! The shepherd shot the old dog but the young dog was shot by MacLeish. Your paper's *wrong*—!

[*He turns and spits in the fire*]

CURTAIN

POEMS

THE DANCERS
INHERIT THE PARTY

for Jessie M. McGuffie

THE DANCERS INHERIT THE PARTY

When I have talked for an hour I feel lousy –
Not so when I have danced for an hour:
The dancers inherit the party
While the talkers wear themselves out and
sit in corners alone, and glower.

ANGLES OF STAMPS

Stick a stamp at an angle on a letter
It means a kiss, yes, but what sort, is it a torn
Kiss, sweet kiss, anguished, cool as water
Rowan-burning kiss or kiss as pure as hawthorn?

Of my typist I asked, she being wise in mythology
Can you tell me, please, the proper angle to denote
To my own true love that I love her most truly
Or do I expect a stamp to say what a kiss cannot?

Sir, she said, I have no experience of your kisses
I have never met you in a meadow, I am just a typist
                              and a simple girl.
A crooked stamp means a kiss and so do little crosses
But whether you love your true love as true as you say
                              only time will tell.

O. H. M. S.

To my creel and stack-net island
Of the little hills, low and dark,
Her Majesty's Government graciously sent
Me an Assistance clerk.

He frowned, 'May I come in?'
– To inspect me, he meant. 'Please do.
I shall sit on this old oil drum
And leave the chair for you.'

'Some questions require to be answered.'
'You must ask me whatever you wish.
– Those things strung on the knotted string
You are staring at, are fish.'

'Fish? – I thought they were socks.'
He wrote me all down in his book.
O little dark island, I brought him, and after
Did you give me a darker look?

DON'T KNOW

Who has hair the colour of toast?
Who is the Found among the Lost?
Who is sweetest when she is most
My Mary?

AH, SO THAT IS WHY

O why do the fishermen wear dark woolly jerseys?
It is to wipe their pens on, my dear.

BEDTIME

So put your nightdress on
It is so white and long
And your sweet night-face
Put it on also please
It is the candle-flame
It is the flame above
Whose sweet shy shame
My love, I love, I love.

NAME POEM

J is for Jessie, wee and tall
E xtravagant dark in silence as
S orrow for all things pass, maternal
S ad for blackbirds, bluebells, grass.
I do such a kind girl call
E , yes, exceptional.

BLACK TOMINTOUL

To Scotland came the tall American
And went to stay on a little farm
Oh it was a Scotch farm set in the wild
A wee Scotch burn and a stoney field

She came to a corner, it was raining
And the little trees were all leaning in
This was Scotland the way she had thought of it
Care, not gravity, makes them lean
The rain falling Scotchly, Scotchly
And the hills that did not soar up but in

But most she looked at the bull so wild
She looked at the bull with the eyes of a child
Never in New York did she see such a bull
As this great Scotch one, Tomintoul
She called him secretly, the great Scotch bull

He was black all over, even for a bull
And oh he had such a lovely hide
She saw him follow one cow aside
Tell me, please, is that cow his bride?

No, they are all his lawful br-r-ride
There were twentyfour cows on the Scotch hillside

It was almost too much for the tall American girl
She watched him stand on his opposite hill
Black Tomintoul, and he always bellowed
But afterwards something in her was mellowed.

FRANK THE BEAR WRITES HIS DEB FRIEND

It is to me, a prisoned pleb
She writes – most thoughtful of a deb.
The problem now ari
– Ses as to frame her a reply.

For frankly I do not
Remember all that I was taught,
Only around the comma
There lingers an aroma

Whose principle I option is
When writing such a letter
The more you have of them the better,
And so it reads like this:

My, dear I hope you're, fine and
Enjoying a kinder, fate
Than I am, here, incarcerate
By, Capitalists. To, hand

Your letter tells me, Hugh
Has joined the Salvation, Army
A thing I never, thought, he'd do
I think he must be, balmy

To chuck it and enlist
My, dear I almost can't
Believe it I'm a, Militant
Anarchist and a, Pacifist

Myself I must stop, there
Hoping that this finds, you
As it leaves, me your old, and, true,
Friend, Frank, the, Bear, , ,

GIFT

How silly and how dear, how very dear
To send a dehydrated porcupine
By letter post, with love. It did appear
That it was such – a gift, but more a sign
Of love, from her I love, that girl of mine.

I did not think it too exceptional
(Acceptance being one part of being in love)
And yet I thought it strange, for you could call
It strange to send a dried-up porcupine
With love. My dear, I thought. O darling mine.

And stroked with love its quills so soft and fine
At which I saw it was not animal
But vegetable. Yes, it was vegetable –
The prickly part of some old hoary pine
She had detached and sent me, plus a line

There scribbled in her dear and silly scrawl:
'I hope it did not prick you, dearest mine,
I did not mean you to be hurt at all.'

ORKNEY INTERIOR

Doing what the moon says, he shifts his chair
Closer to the stove and stokes it up
With the very best fuel, a mixture of dried fish
And tobacco he keeps in a bucket with crabs

Too small to eat. One raises its pincer
As if to seize hold of the crescent moon
On the calendar which is almost like a zodiac
With inexplicable and pallid blanks. Meanwhile

A lobster is crawling towards the clever
Bait that is set inside the clock
On the shelf by the wireless – an inherited dried fish
Soaked in whisky and carefully trimmed

With potato flowers from the Golden Wonders
The old man grows inside his ears.
Click! goes the clock-lid, and the unfortunate lobster
Finds itself a prisoner inside the clock,

An adapted cuckoo-clock. It shows no hours, only
Tides and moons and is fitted out
With two little saucers, one of salt and one of water
For the lobster to live on while, each quarter-tide,

It must stick its head through the tiny trapdoor
Meant for the cuckoo. It will be trained to read
The broken barometer and wave its whiskers
To Scottish Dance Music, till it grows too old.

Then the old man will have to catch himself another lobster.
Meanwhile he is happy and takes the clock
Down to the sea. He stands and oils it
In a little rock pool that reflects the moon.

FRENCH POEM

La vie, la vie
Beaucoup de parapluies.

A U T H O R ised translation:
O life, what a lot of
Umbrellas.

CELTIC POEM
for Derry MacDiarmid

Lovely the stars shine over Galway
Where I go walking with thee, with thee.
Then take me back and my harp along with me –
I am yours forever, wee Bonnie Dundee!

GLASGOW POEM

Airship poet Guillaume (Angel) Apollinaire
Wrote poetry something rer.
It was back in the Future. What the Scotch call 'auld Sol'
He called the 'sun airplane'. It would drive you up the wall.

OPTIMIST

My would-be father, old and slow,
Did buy himself a kind of tin
– Can for brewing proper, out-of-door tea in.
The bloody fire, though, it wouldn't go.

It was the bloody wet sticks, and everything.
Alone he kneeled on the out-of-door grass,
Blowing with love. I remember how, home again,
He brewed wild tea on the domestic gas.

MILK BOTTLES

Tell a man's true state by how
He deals with his milk bottles. I remember
Once I was having a good time
And I had none at all, while now
(Lodged here August – mid-December)
The milk firm's missing 159.

ARCHIE, THE LYRICAL LAMPLIGHTER

From pillar to post goes the sad young writer.
Shall I be, will I be, a lamplighter?
A wife and five weans to feed is not a joke.

Better, better for my literary soul
Would have been Assistance, but They handed me a pole
And they said, Soldier on! Or something. So that's the story.

Also they gave me a little Corpy cap.
It makes me feel like Hamlet and I *do* care a rap
(Whatever a rap is). It is not at all a joke.

It is not at all a joke to be an employee
Of the Glasgow Corporation, and I say, See me –
I could crown Them with this pole and that ain't no story.

From lamppost to post goes the sad young writer.
His soul is very dark although his way is lighter.
One-o-five unwritten stories on your mind is not a joke.

THE WRITER AND BEAUTY

The best a writer writes is Beautiful.
He should ignore the Mad and Dutiful.

Meanwhile, of course, the Lie is there,
The posh Lie struts in the social air

And writers write it, and it is
Part of the analyst's neurosis.

Well, a writer should defy
It. A writer writes of sky

And other things quite sad and Beautiful.
He should ignore the Mad and Dutiful.

See how lame and blind he goes.
See how he dances on his toes!

FINLAY'S HOUSE (IN ROUSAY)

And this is Finlay's house –
A wild stone on the floor,
Lots and lots of books
And a chair where you can't sit for
– No, not the tar –
The hooks, the lost fish-hooks.

Dried fish festoon the wall
And that stone sticks the door.
Spiders spin in nooks.
The visitors tend to fall:
They trip first, then they fall –
They catch on the lost fish-hooks.

I ought to shift that stone
But it seems easier
To unscrew the door.
Am I an awful man?
I'm better housed than ducks
And like to lose fish-hooks.

THE CHIEF CROP OF ORKNEY

As everyone is well aware, the chief crop of Orkney
                              is wireless-poles
But do you remember the year of the *short* wireless-poles?
                              It occurred
Within living memory. A lack of quarter-moons.
                              Some poor old souls
Were unable to get Radio Luxembourg, or even the
                              Light, but only the Third.

PROBLEMS OF AN ORKNEY HOUSEWIFE

What with the dirty weather
And all, you really can't
Keep a clean moon these days.
We have to polish ours THREE times a week.

BI-LINGUAL POEM

Christmas, how your cold sad face
Leans on the city where everything glows.
Far in the fields stands the gentle animal.
Quel a pity il so seldom snows.

ANGELS

When we are dead we will all be angels
And we will see how many of us can balance on a pin.
I think we may manage seven or eight of us
Angelically balanced, if we all squeeze in.

ISLAND MOMENT

In the still of an island evening
She goes to the big shed
Which is where she keeps the herring.
The sun – and their eyes – are red.

Past the War Memorial cycles
Her son who – O delight –
Is newly married and may count
That chest's sweet hairs now every night.

He is brown, and very tall.
If one believes the rumour
The island sculled itself to Kirkwall
Using him, Big Jim, as an oar.

Dusk is in the shed.
The long white boat is hers.
Also the yellow bamboo wand
For fishing sillocks, lithe and cuithes.

And the little herring barrel.
The light just strikes it over
Islands and miles and miles of water
That tilts to the North Pole.

The lady of the island shop has to go to the shore-side shed for salted herrings. It is sunset, and her son who is newly married (and is a little set for her) is cycling home after being at the lobsters. The hairs are on his wife's chest: you can imagine, I hope, that he might find them worth the counting.

CASTLES

One man is chosen king of every castle
Whose bricks are soft as snow or crumbling clay.
Embedded in them here and there's a thistle.
The game is for a June or July day.

The others have to stay below the castle.
Like servants or like slaves they never say
It's their turn to be kings. Can they not wrestle?
They should have shots at each, alternately.

The kings, however, also build the castle.
The work is slow and serious – and gay.
Whole hordes of castles harden as they settle.
The kings leap down and land in moats of hay.

JESS

I like Jess
The more because
She furs my ears,
She shines my paws.

Strange that dark
Can be so fair.
Animals
Have also hair.

THE ISLAND BEASTS WAIT FOR THE BOAT

The island boat is a toy
Or else, as a little foal
Is all long legs, I see it all
Tall masts, with but ONE funnel.

A disappointment. Well . . .
Oh dear, why must we wait
In this long queue in the snow? I moo
This move's unfortunate.

And I can't see through that porthole.
Still, it's something to have your skin.
Yes, warm your hands if you want to. Whew,
I wouldn't wear an oilskin for *any*thing . . .

TWO VARIATIONS ON AN ORKNEY THEME, WITH NOTES
for Ernest Marwick

(The Shetlander is a fisherman by day and a crofter by night while the Orcadian is a crofter by day and a fly-by-night)

A budgerigar in a cage
Puts all Orkney in a rage.
Orkney knows a budgie ought
To be inside a lobster-pot.

(But nowadays the lobsters grow little propellors and find a ready market with B.O.A.C.)

A lobstercopter in a cage
Puts all Orkney in a rage.
Orkney knows a copter ought
To be inside an aero-pot.

JOHN SHARKEY IN ROUSAY
(OR, THE WILD ANGEL BOY)

Quack-quack he called the silly man
To far-off ducks   And fired
Alas his boss's caravan
By Accident   Attired

In flame it graced the highest hill
Six stalwart farmers threw
Chill water   (chiefly over him
Crying Cock-a-doodle-doo)

Till in the dawn it stood a hulk
Dramatic   Barnacles
Of hail on it came pelting down
Cufuffle round it ruled

While he Tra-la gave not a damn
He was far more dismayed
That almost every Ba-ba-lamb
Of pure white wool was made.

CATCH

There once was a fisherman of Scrabster
Caught in his pot a gey queer lapster.

Thought he, this lapster's a sure sellar,
A tail it has, and a wee propellor,

In fact, it's no ordinary lapster felly,
It looks far more like a peedie heli –

You know yon kind of hoverlapster,
A what do you call it, helicapster.

Aye, aye, it's a peedie helicapster:
There's lots are caught in the sea off Scrabster.

ORKNEY LYRICS

1. Peedie Mary Considers the Sun

The peedie sun is not so tall
He walks on golden stilts
Across, across, across the water
But I have darker hair.

2. The English Colonel Explains an Orkney Boat

The boat swims full of air.
You see, it has a point at both
Ends, sir, somewhat
As lemons. I'm explaining

The hollowness is amazing. That's
The way a boat
Floats.

3. Mansie Considers Peedie Mary

Peedie Alice Mary is
My cousin, so we cannot kiss.
And yet I love my cousin fair:
She wears her seaboots with such an air.

*'Peedie' is the Orkney word for 'wee'. Many Orkney girls have two
Christian names, and many Orkney men are called 'Mansie', which is the
diminutive of 'Magnus'.*

4. Mansie Considers the Sea in the Manner of Hugh MacDiarmid

The sea, I think, is lazy,
It just obeys the moon
– All the same I remember what Engels said:
'Freedom is the consciousness of necessity'.

5. Folk Song for Poor Peedie Mary

Peedie Mary
Bought a posh
Big machine
To do her wash.

Peedie Mary
Stands and greets,
Where dost thoo
Put in the peats?

Silly Peedie
Mary thoo
Puts the peats
Below, baloo.

Peedie Mary
Greets the more,
What did the posh paint
Come off for?

6. John Sharkey is Pleased to be in Sourin at Evening

How beautiful, how beautiful, the mill
– Wheel is not turning though the waters spill
Their single tress. The whole old mill
Leans to the West, the breast.

TWICE

(Once)

It is a little pond
And it is frail and round

And it is in the wood,
A doleful mood

Of birches (white) and stale
Very old thin rain grown pale.

(Twice)

It is a little pond
And it is brown; around

It (like the eye
Of a cow) soft emerald

Grasses and things
Grow up. The tall white harlequins

Sway again
And again, in the bright new clean rain.

SPRING HOLIDAY

The holiday stares at the sky
With a blind white eye.

It is bright. It is whiter than Sunday.
A daisy's. That cat's on the wall.

Part of the flashing of light
Off the infinite invisible brassbands.

White. Bright. Awful.
Even the clouds are wrong.

DARK MORNING FOR SCAREY MARY

How lone and dark my morning is.
Things clangs and is all scarey.
I don't think *that's* a dairy.
Mary, you never s A w a fairy.
Hold tight to dearest Elvis.

ART STUDENT

So neat, so compact in your trousers
It almost staggers me you are alive
A little miracle as the poets say springs are
Made complete, where do they come from, your eyes

And your hair (in a pony-tail) and all intensely
You, little student, walking whole
Into our lives as flowers from underground
Sudden as April primroses, so

Beauty, it seems, is simply factual
You have no need of us though you hugged in tears
A little grief, or in sweet pyjamas
Wept for a frost that had to be

For we could never distress you *really*
Nor bend the straight street where you go
Carrying your neat dreams tied in ribbons
Like all the drawings in your portfolio.

SNOW
by Tatsuji Miyoshi

Sending Taro to sleep – it slowly blankets Taro's roof.
Sending Jiro to sleep – it slowly blankets Jiro's roof.

from *The Poetry of Living Japan*

SNOW IN ROUSAY

Sending Mansie to sleep – it slowly blankets Peedie
                                    Mary's roof.

Sending Peedie Mary to sleep – it slowly blankets
                                    Mansie's roof.

SCENE

The fir tree stands quite still and angles
On the hill, for green Triangles.

Stewing in its billy there
The tea is strong, and brown, and Square.

The rain is Slant. Soaked fishers sup
Sad Ellipses from a cup.

POET

At night, when I cannot sleep,
I count the islands
And I sigh when I come to Rousay
– My dear black sheep.

END OF A HOLIDAY

My father climbs the stairs
Above my head
And then I hear him climb
Into his bed.

Sheep bleat – the sun's last sparks
Float through the wood
Like bubbles in last week's
Old lemonade.

I wait, and then I ask
Is he all right
Up in the dark without
A proper light?

He pulls the heavy clothes
Up to his chin.
I'm fine, he says, I'm perfect.
– Goodnight, son.

THE ONE-HORSE TOWN

A little one-horse town . . . I asked, 'Where
is this?' The Sheriff told me, 'Dobbin.'
The evening sun went down.

THE TUG

Where the fishers wait for bites
Toots the little tug – in tights!

Round each river bend and loop
TOOT – like through a circus-hoop.

The Towns say Tut, that boat's not black,
It's far more like a Union Jack!

The Steadings never even peep
Because they are all fast asleep!

So on and on, for hours and hours . . .
The sky is blue, each bank's all flowers.

And when for Tea the Captain whistles
The crew sit down to spangled rissoles!

GLASGOW BEASTS, AN A BURD HAW, AN INSEKS, AN, AW, A FUSH

PAPERCUTS BY JOHN PICKING
& PETE McGINN

a wee buik fir big weans

tae Shimpei Kusano
whae writ
a haill buik o poems
aboot puddocks
'The Hundredth Class'

that's us

noo read oan

an mind yir back

see me
wan time
ah wis a fox
an wis ah sleekit! ah
gaed slinkin
            heh
an snappin
            yeh
the blokes
aa sayed ah wis a G R E A T fox
aw nae kiddin
ah wis pretty good
had a whole damn wood
in them days
hen

an wan time
ah wis a moose
a richt wee douce
chap
Maw
kep sayin
haw
hint
it
awful
an
it's
aa
a
trap

chums
this time
ah wis a bed-bug
Dostoevsky
yelly caurs
cawd
Haw Desire
an
here wee me

anither
time
ah wis a
minnie
aw
the pond
haw
the shoogly caur
gaun
see s
a frond
fir
ma wee jaur

an wance
ah wis a zebra
heh heh
crossin

syne
ah wis a midgie
neist a stank
foon that kin o
thankless
didjye
ever
spen
a
hail simmer
stottin
up
an
doon

hooch
a heilan coo
wis mair liker
it
        the hiker
s
hoo hoos
ferr feart
o ma
herr-do

an wance
ah wis a budgie
        like
Wee Davie
123
Garscadden Road
(oot Polmadie)

honess
pals
like
no been born
a cleg
s e bess

ho
it wis a laugh
been
a giraffe like
ma neck
goat sneckit
in this tree
so ah says
haw Sara
an she says whit
way ur ye staunin
aa bandy-leggit?
bandy-leggit
ah says
so help me
get
yir
giraffe
free

come back
as a coal-hoarse
ho the
      heavy
an
hauf the day
wi yir piece
hauf-etten
hung
roon yir
ear

UNCOLLECTED POEMS

FISHING FROM THE BACK OF ROUSAY

Iceland, they say, is nearest. There, the waves
Originate, and roll – like rolling graves –
Towards these umber cliffs. Green seaweed paves

Like sloppy ice (but slippier) the stairs
Of rock you must descend. Then what impairs
Your fall down fifteen flights to lobster-lairs

Is only, now and then, a limpet's hand
So small and rough, and clenched. And where you stand
When you have reached the foot, is not dry land.

For one by one the rollers rise and swell
And swell some more, and swell: you cannot tell
If this will fall (Boom) where the last one fell

Or (Crash) on your own head. But, bait your hook
And cast in a deep channel; while you look
You're left to fish in a salt-water brook

That fills till it's Atlantic. Fine, you sigh,
A bite at any minute. Where's the sky?
Boom, Boom, it says, you're drowned! – Then it's rolled by.

POEM ON MY POEM ON HER AND THE HORSE

A little horse came treading through the snow
At which she said, Poor horse, poor horse thou art
Poor little horse to have that heavy cart,
To have that cart, to have to make it go.

And then I thought, Oho, I thought, Oho
She's thinking of her own small saddest part.
Poor horse. Poor horse. Poor horse. Poor horse. Poor cart.
And in her eyes the snow, you know, the snow.

SUCH IS THE WORLD

Lookin doon
Thro the leaves o a tree
– Green leaves
In the evenin –
We seen a laddie
Wi his dog, a black mongrel,
Bi the bairns' bonfire.

An the fire
Wis deein doon
An the serious laddie
Wis aa alane there,
Aa alane,
An the mongrel gaed
Tae an fro,
Here an there,
Tae be sniffin, wi
Wee black feet.

Aa this we seen
Thro the leaves o a tree in
The evenin – aye, 'such'
Says Zukofsky
'Is the world'.

Wan wee fragment frae Louis Zukofsky
pit intae Glasgow-Scots:

ZUKOFSKY
(frae 'A'
1–12)

– It was such a muggy day
The carpenter was ready to paint.
The laundryman said
He heard over TV
A layer of cold air
From Canada
Was rolling our way.
I felt like asking
Were they going to show it.

FINLAY

– It wis sic a close day
The jiner wis hammerin.
The orra-man sayed
He seen oan The Telly
A puckle cauld air
Frae Scrabster
Wis chairgin wir way.
I feeled like speirin, Here
Wis it oan the noo.

orra-man – odd job man
Scrabster – tiny port in far north of Scotland
speiring – questioning, but with dark Scotch undertones!

LUCKY

I first read Tolstoy's 'The Snow-Blizzard'
In a wooden shed with
A big one blowing in.
– It was cold in bed!

And I first read Turgenev's 'First Love'
By a candle
In a whitewashed out-house. (Raining)
– What an apple-y smell!

THE VILLAGE BAKER

His clothes are mushroom-white. He
Shines all night.

Trad
-Itional bread-smells rise
By his red eyes,

Through bars
Past pines
To stars,

To star-
Ry skies.

MIDHOPE (ALL GONE)

My father in his meadow
– Lovely shadow

Of the beech woods – and the pigeons
Going coo

– Coo roo coo
Like quicksilver

– And the milestone:
'3 miles to Society' – we

Never got so far.

DALCHONZIE

Hot day

        the pines say Wheesht!
        along the railway

  Night

the mill has two wheels, a red, a black – one
                        is the sun.

Wheesht is what the
Scotch say, meaning
Hush, or Be Quiet)

Bibliography

Abrioux, Yves *Ian Hamilton Finlay: a visual primer* (2nd ed.) (London: Reaktion, 1992)

Finlay, Ian Hamilton (ed.) *Poor.Old.Tired.Horse*, nos 1–25, 1961–67

Finlay, Ian Hamilton *The Dancers Inherit the Party & Glasgow Beasts an a Burd* (Edinburgh: Polygon, 1996)

Finlay, Ian Hamilton *The Dancers Inherit the Party* (Worcester: Migrant Press, 1960)

Finlay, Ian Hamilton *Glasgow beasts, an a burd, an haw, an inseks, an aw, a fush* (Edinburgh: Wild Flounder Press, 1961)

Finlay, Ian Hamilton *The Sea-Bed and other stories* (Edinburgh: Castle Wynd Printers, 1958)

Henderson, Hamish *The Armstrong Nose: Selected Letters of Hamish Henderson*, ed. Alec Finlay (Edinburgh: Polygon, 1996)

MacCaig, Norman (ed.) *Honour'd shade: an anthology of new Scottish poetry to mark the bicentenary of the birth of Robert Burns* (Edinburgh: Chambers, 1959)

MacDiarmid, Hugh *Albyn: Shorter Books and Monographs*, ed. Alan Riach (Manchester: Carcanet, 1996). *See* 'the ugly birds without wings', pp. 318–31

MacDiarmid, Hugh *New Selected Letters*, ed. Grieve, Edwards and Riach (Manchester: Carcanet, 2001)

Morgan, Edwin *Crossing the Border: Essays on Scottish Literature* (Manchester: Carcanet, 1990). See 'Early Finlay', pp. 292–299

New English Dramatists 14 (Harmondsworth: Penguin, 1970). Includes 'Walking Through Seaweed' and 'The Estate Hunters'; with an Introduction by Edwin Morgan

Sheeler, Jessie *Little Sparta: The Garden of Ian Hamilton Finlay* (London: Frances Lincoln, 2003)

Stanford, Derek *Inside the Forties: Literary Memoirs 1937–1957* (London: Sidgwick & Jackson 1977)

POLYGON is an imprint of Birlinn Limited. Our list includes titles by Alexander McCall Smith, Liz Lochhead, Kenneth White, Robin Jenkins and other critically acclaimed authors. Should you wish to be put on our catalogue mailing list contact:

Catalogue Request
Polygon
West Newington House
10 Newington Road
Edinburgh EH9 1QS
Scotland, UK

Tel: +44 (0) 131 668 4371
Fax: +44 (0) 131 668 4466
e-mail: info@birlinn.co.uk

Postage and packing is free within the UK. For overseas orders, postage and packing (airmail) will be charged at 30% of the total order value.

Our complete list can be viewed on our website. Go to www.birlinn.co.uk and click on the Polygon logo at the top of the home page.